Death Valley: An Ongoing Exploration

The Paintings of Janet Morgan and Gregory Frux

Death Valley National Park Visitor Center, April 2012

An Art and Adventures Publication

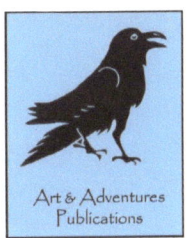

An Art and Adventures Publication 2012

Second printings, 2015

Artandadventures.com

Dedicated to the Park Service Staff at Death Valley National Park

Table of Contents

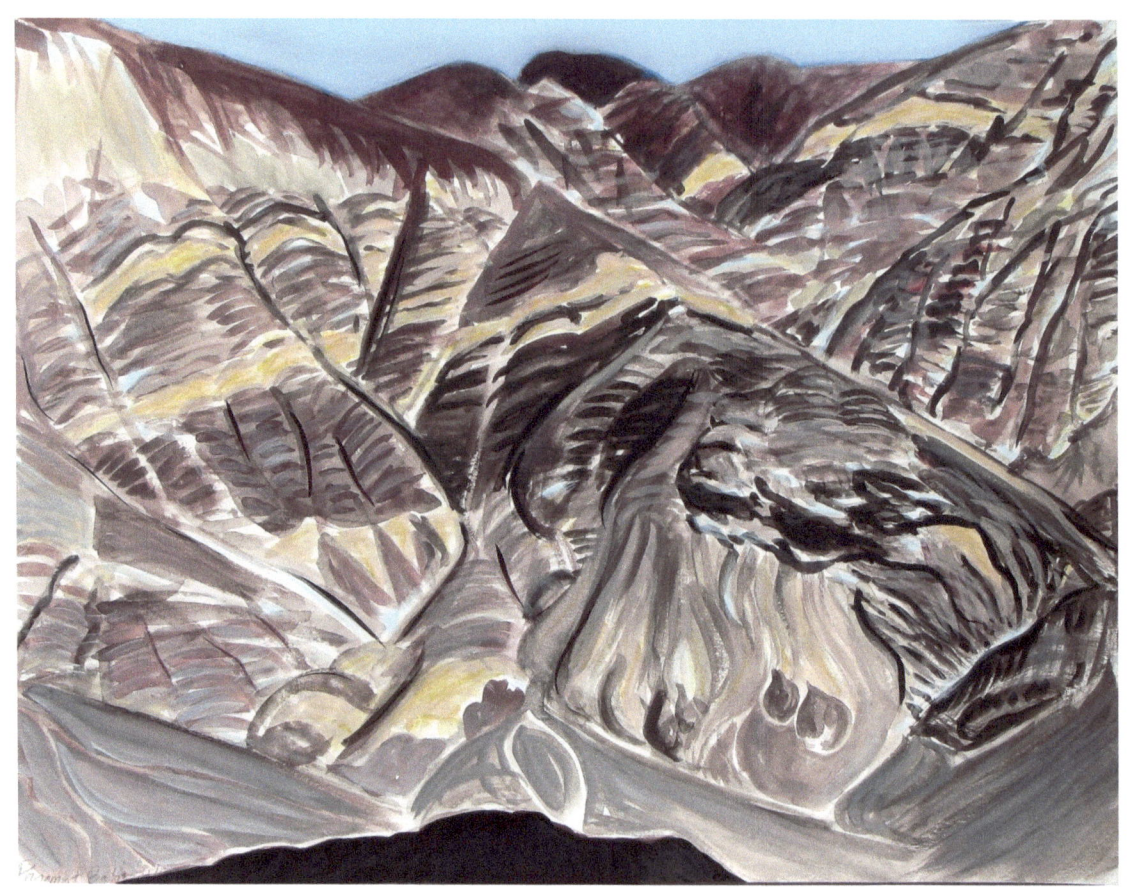

Panamint Butte 2008 watercolor 15" x 20" Janet Morgan

Introduction

In the 1870s Hudson River School painters like Thomas Moran and Albert Bierstadt played a critical role in documenting the landscapes of the West. It was through their works of art that the public came to see the first views of Yellowstone and Yosemite. Their efforts led to the world's first national parks.

Death Valley National Park is no different. For generations artists -- painters, photographers, musicians and cinematographers -- have been inspired by the immense scale, the stark and alien landscape, the raw, exposed earthly elements, while at the same time dazzled by the fine detail of the desert captured in the color of small flowers and shy critters often overlooked and lost in the vastness of Death Valley.

Art means many things to many people. Art can be a skill one acquires through experience, study or observation (e.g. the art of rock climbing). It is also the conscious use of skills and creative imagination one uses in the production of aesthetic objects. Artists have employed their skills for centuries as a means of capturing and conveying their thoughts and feelings about every topic under the sun.

The first depictions of the Valley were of a harsh, unforgiving and deathly place. These were images recounted from a group of people who suffered at the hands of an environment they did not understand. Those who followed, prepared to deal with the limits of the desert, saw the beauty and majesty this land possesses. Like so many artists of the past, today's artists, including Janet Morgan and Greg Frux, provide a way for the public to see the park differently, to experience the park in new ways. In turn this allows you to become more curious and more engaged in the stewardship of these special lands we call National Parks.

Terry Baldino, Chief of Interpretation & Education at Death Valley National Park, retired in 2014 following 35 years of government service.

Companions in Life, Travel and Art: Janet Morgan and Gregory William Frux

Death Valley is the farthest place on Earth from most popular visions of Eden. Its homicidal vastness forbids most life from taking root, destroying many foolish or reckless enough to defy its terrible splendor. Picturesque America is sublimely enamored with the landscape of desolation and destruction. A caldera spouting geysers and boiling hot springs at the headwaters of the *Roche Jaune* was first known as "Coulter's Hell" after its eponymous discoverer, John Coulter, fur-trapper and veteran of Lewis and Clark's *Corps of Discovery*. The river's name was inspired by volcanic sulfur deposits along its banks. In 1872 President Grant signed legislation that created Yellowstone National Park, which erupted into a Western tourism boom that shows no signs of abating.

Americans have always been enamored of Romantic landscapes, drawn to places that inspire terror, awe and wonder. The Great Dismal Swamp, straddling the boundary between Virginia and North Carolina, is anything but doleful. Rather, it is a popular passage along the Atlantic Intracoastal Waterway. Vacationers and honeymooners drawn to Niagara's thundering cascade might glimpse well-coopered daredevils being devoured by the mist. The promise of adventure might be fulfilled by the precipitous grandeur of Grand Canyon or coming face-to-face with ravenous bears that stalk the hostile beauty of Alaska's Arctic fringe. Adventure abides in places where the shadow of death brightens life's flame.

The history of the American West is full of dynamic duos like Meriwether Lewis and William Clark, Charles Bent and Cerain St. Vrain, and power-couples like John Charles and Jessie Benton Frémont, and Seth and Mary Eastman to name but a few. Soldiers, explorers, scouts and trappers who explored wild places and tamed the frontier must share credit for the canonical image of the West with the couples and families who made it their home, and likewise shoulder the burden of guilt for displacing First Nations in the process. More than one power-couple like Marcus and Narcissa Whitman perished in the Native blowback to Euro-American expansionism. In a mythical sense, frontiersmen and adventurers fulfilled human destiny by venturing into the wilderness to regain Paradise, and thus create a New World.

Today Janet Morgan and Gregory William Frux embody the spirit of nineteenth-century artist explorers, trekking the globe from Hudson Valley to Tierra del Fuego, from Morocco to the Arctic

Circle. To quote Frux:

> I feel heir to 19th century scientists and artist who pushed the boundaries of exploration. My journal keeping is a major aspect of my artistic practice and reflects the unmediated first impressions which are foundational to my creative output.

Like predecessors Thomas Moran, Albert Bierstadt and Eliza Greatorex, Frux and Morgan have set up their permanent base in New York City. Travels to far-flung destinations, from the Polar regions to North Africa, South America and Death Valley emulate historic figures such as William Hodges, Samuel Seymour, John James Audubon, George Catlin, the Kern brothers, Karl Bodmer, Seth Eastman and Frederic Church.

Frux was a shipboard artist on cruises to Arctic Norway. Both Frux and Morgan have traveled to Antarctica and done artist residencies with the National Park Service at Death Valley and Weir Farm. Additionally, Frux was resident-artist at Glacier and Joshua Tree National Parks.

Morgan was artist-in-residence at New York's Omega Institute where she exhibited work in The Women and Power Conference, and for nearly two decades Morgan worked as an art therapist with adult cancer patients at Sloan Kettering Cancer Center. She now gives workshops for the Hudson River Pageant produced by Earth Celebrations.

Both Frux and Morgan work thematically, uniting diverse interests such as travel, health and spirituality. Drawing inspiration from rambles in the Shawangunk Mountains or trekking the Bolivian Andes, Morgan and Frux approach art-making in ways that are physically demanding and rooted in athleticism. Morgan trained as a dancer. Frux has long been devoted to rock-climbing and mountaineering. Apart from landscape-based imagery, Morgan's figurative work celebrates the spirituality of nature, common ground shared with many in their circle of friends including visionary artists Alex and Allison Grey. She has exhibited at the now-famous Burning Man festivals. To quote Morgan's artist's statement:

> ...how we are and how we move and think comes from the land. I have also created a pantheon of nearly 200 gods and goddesses. While painting their portraits, their territories and lands, temples and terrains, became revealed. This opened up the desire in me to paint portraits of our land, deserts and mountains, the things that shape us and open us up to the sacred. The movement in the land is a dance - carving and pushing up and sweeping away...

Morgan's painting style is fluid, gestural and energetic. Composed in sweeping arcs reminiscent of the aerial landscapes of Dr. Atl, *Badwater Shadows* (see page 11) was painted in the early morning to let Morgan work in the shade. Badwater is the lowest, hottest and driest place in North America, and yet snow is frequently visible on the 11,000-foot summit of Telescope Peak across the valley. Roads circle to avoid the fans while a foot-path leads down to salt flats in the lowest elevation accessible by tourists. *Out of Cottonwood Canyon – Kit Fox Hills and the Death Valley Buttes* (see page 17) was painted from the mouth of Cottonwood Canyon, a distance of many miles from the Death Valley Buttes. Distinct calligraphic brushstrokes echo Morgan's description of terrain as a dance, suggesting perhaps a debt to American artists like Charles Burchfield or Marsden Hartley.

Panamint Butte (see page 31) was Morgan's third attempt to paint the 10,000- foot vertical stack of sediment, behind which an even greater number of layers bend back upon itself. Following its falling layers in reverse leads one back to Death Valley. Grey-violet formations punctuated with yellow flow downward like a floppy blossom, reminiscent of O'Keeffe.

Frux paints with a more deliberate and scientific eye. Morgan's ecstatic vision of nature is balanced by a sobriety of observation embraced by Frux.

Based on fieldwork, oil sketches and photography, *The End of Nature* (see page 13) is a studio picture counter-intuitively composed in a vertical format that represents a long, narrow view across the valley floor, above which Telescope Peak and the Panamint Range tower over great alluvial fans, dwarfing a stranded solitary motorist. The tight-knit sense of form, the emphasis on line nods again to O'Keeffe, but there is also a determined tangibility recalling Edward Hopper.

In *Narrows, Cottonwood Canyon* (see page 15) we find an example of Frux's fieldwork. According to the artist, this oil painting on masonite represents the navigable limit of an airport rental car, beyond which a rugged four-wheeler is required to reach the cottonwood groves, rumored feral burros and mountain sheep. The composition is organized around abstract geometries suggested by canyon walls. A dark ferrous-black triangle crashes into the right-hand edge of the frame, riding a blue dagger across pale hues. As in *The End of Nature*, the point of view is earthbound, the very opposite of Morgan's soaring vistas.

Another painting in oil on panel *Road Cut, Death Valley* (see page 18) uses Frux's field-working methods to assemble a studio painting from memory and photographic references. The image records a visit to the site by geology students who investigate layers of millions-years old lake-bed sediment and subsequent lava deposits along a road cut seen from below.

Frux sinks his perspective below the common surface like Death Valley itself, which he uses to demonstrate the

diminishing returns of mechanized transportation, a metaphor for human mortality projected against the vast, endless but mutable indifference of nature. According to Morgan, "...the land is sacred... it is our home."

While Frux elaborates on these maxims:

> Inhabiting this extraordinary planet with unprecedented access to remote areas, tools to delve deeper into the richness of the world and time and resource to do it I am faced with a sense of wonder and celebration.

Artistically, if not stylistically, Frux and Morgan are soul-mates—neo-Romanticists whose work draws on the power of nature not only to inspire, but to instruct. A force that shapes the banal realities of the physical world, Nature also possesses the transformative capacity to overcome them as a guidebook, a temple of life and a path to wisdom.

by James Lancel McElhinney © 2012

James Lancel McElhinney received a Master of Fine Arts Degree from Yale University School of Art. He is a visual artist and writer who teaches at Pratt Institute and at the Art Students League of New York. McElhinney has published two books on drawing. He conducts oral history interviews for the Smithsonian Archives of American Art and a number of foundations. McElhinney has spoken to audiences at the Museum of Modern Art, New York Historical Society, The United States Air Force Academy, various National Park Service sites including Cedar Grove: Thomas Cole House, Bent's Old Fort and Harper's Ferry where he was once artist-in-residence. McElhinney lives in Manhattan and in the Hudson Valley with his wife, art historian Dr. Katherine E. Manthorne. His biography is published in the 2012 edition of *Who's Who is America*.

Death Valley Seeing

    Cook-stove and pots, canteens and ski poles rattle as our SUV clatters up the alluvial fan, following a barely-there path, jouncing from rut to rock, scraping past thorny shrubs. You might think we were on a dangerous wilderness expedition and you'd be right up to a point. But as we maneuver into the lee of faint shade and pull packs, boots and food bags out for our hike, paint-boxes, brushes, paper and panels also emerge from the tangle of gear. Just another day in the life of painters Gregory Frux and Janet Morgan.

    Over two separate Aprils in 2006 and 2008, I was privileged to join Greg and Janet as a guest writer for their artist-in-residences at Death Valley National Park. Along the way, I was schooled by them and by the diverse landscapes we encountered in the art of Death Valley seeing.

    Hiking the dry stream bed trail into McElvoy Canyon (see page 34) in the Inyo Mountains, I'm reminded of a something I learned as we first drove towards the park. For much of its course, the nearby Mojave River runs underground, invisible to the naked eye but permeating the substrate of desert life. Death Valley can be like that, with complex biotic and geologic happenings obscured from casual view. To fill in the gaps, one must learn to see deeply and imagine grandly: vision and envision. Like the Mojave River, there is a current of life that meanders just below the surface in Death Valley. Small rivulets perhaps, when compared to Pacific Northwest rain forest or Midwest prairie, but no less significant. Perhaps the apparent absence of something makes one look harder for its occurrence — one of the fundamental lessons of Death Valley seeing.

    As Greg and Janet set up to paint, I hike further up canyon. A ways up, I encounter an Inyo snow melt stream. As I kneel to touch cool water to my face, a blast of sound nearly bowls me over. I glance up as a military plane screams down the canyon and out over Saline Valley, a subject later captured in Greg's painting *Death Valley Jet* (see page 6). Death Valley's lessons continue as the roar fades. Contradictions abound: modernity streaks through antiquity, spaciousness and timelessness soon swallow both.

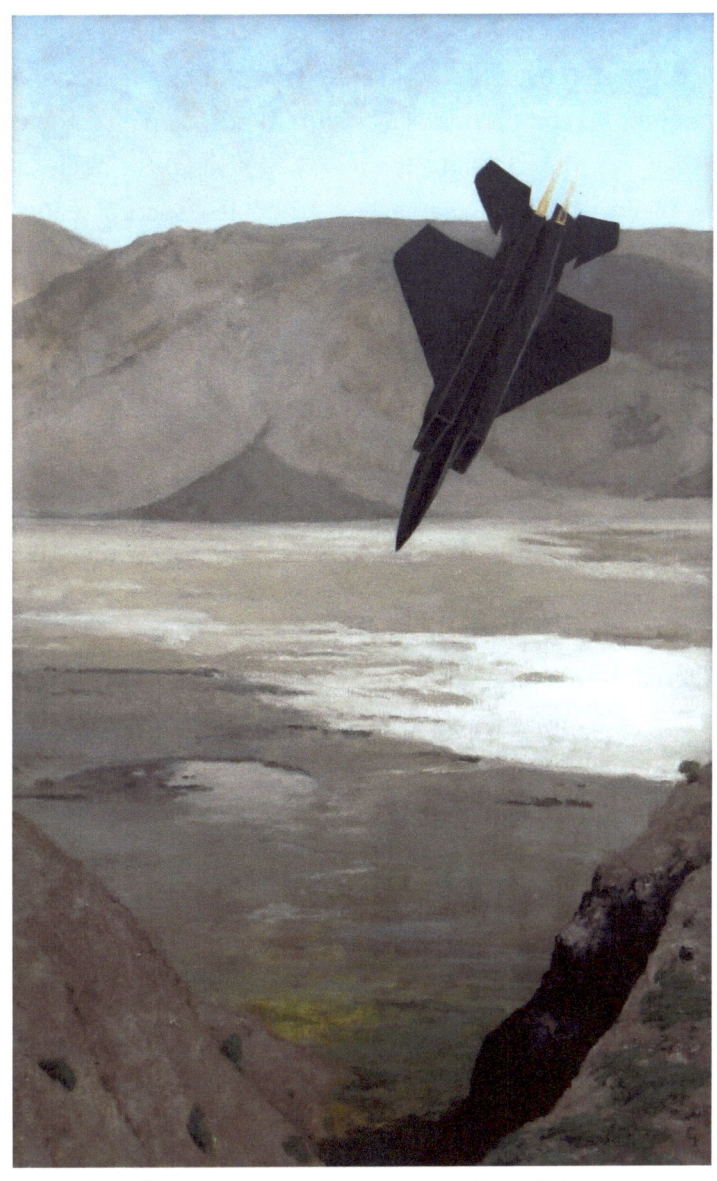

Death Valley Jet, 2007 oil on canvas 36" x 22" Gregory Frux

I reach the first set of McElvoy Canyon falls, veering precipitously down sheer basalt. Scattering mist diamonds, the wind and sun cast ephemeral rainbows. Bubbles meander across a standing pool at the base. For a moment, I stand perpendicular to the falls, turning my head from teeming falls habitat to empty blue sky and muted plains. It's a way of seeing I've been taught by Janet. In her watercolor *Up and Down Golden Canyon* (see page 25), her view soars in a 360 degree arc, capturing the contrast between open vista and secluded containment.

*

But not all lessons emerge from rare and remote settings. Engaging wildlife sightings and intriguing work occur within walking range of our Furnace Creek tent site: a lone coyote streaks across the golf course; overhead, a congregation of ravens gather each noon in the palms. Just before sunrise, several dozen vultures wheel and spin out of a copse of trees and split off on their daily rounds. Amid the bustle of Furnace Creek, Janet sets up under the trees and paints (see page 21). Greg takes his journal out and sketches. We strike out from camp on foot at first light and again at day's end, finding uncommon vistas in common places. Wilderness is not just out there somewhere, but ever close at hand.

These ways of seeing – being still while seeing far, patiently looking close at hand while envisioning hidden places – seem especially necessary when encountering the vast geological expanse of Death Valley. One morning we drive to Zabriskie Point (see page 39) before first light. Janet captures the rapidly evolving colors in quickly rendered watercolors. Greg points out to me various geological features, illustrated in his journal with meticulous hand. Later, we descend to Golden Canyon via Gower Gulch (see page 27). We pause frequently at the revealed strata, running our hands along bumps and striations. Up close, the information we've read in the guidebooks comes alive. Geologists, on some level, must be visionaries. It's no accident that Greg and Janet were invited to accompany geology field school faculty and students from Brooklyn College to Death Valley in 2009.

*

As much as these are landscapes made of time, they are also formed of light and color. Each passing hour casts a unique palette. Days later, we hike up Golden Canyon (see page 23) with park visitors who have signed up for Janet's watercolor workshop. In such places, there is a calculus of necessary shade and effervescent light. Greg and Janet have learned to solve that equation.

I stay for setup then leave the group to strike up canyon. As I navigate a narrowing side trail, the rising walls speak to me. Their bulk tells of their antediluvian upthrust, their steepness and scattered boulders of the immense power of infrequent waters, their variegated strata chants a periodic chart of mineralized stories. At trail's end I clamber further up the tilted rock face to a vista back over Badwater Basin. There, as afternoon light teases new colors from surrounding stone and hazy basin, I take out my journal and sketch all that I can see.

*

I have traveled with Greg and Janet for over two decades. One of their enduring gifts has been introducing me to otherworldly landscapes. We set up one afternoon at Ubehebe Crater (see page 37-38), the site of an ancient volcanic explosion. Ubehebe, a deep pit rimmed by inhospitable cinder and ash, is a harsh place to paint but a remarkable one to experience. The unforgiving sun summons a neon display of reds, oranges and purples. Greg and Janet rig shade from the blasting sun and a tentative awning from the driving wind and produce equally remarkable paintings.

Later, Janet and I wander off to explore trails around the rim. In a bland stretch of cinder, tipped by a subtle blush of color missed by most, we hunker down to an expanse of pale pink and blue wildflowers reaching tentatively out of the gray and black, a phenomenon that Janet calls "belly flowers." Though our eyes are drawn to the obvious beauty, Death Valley teaches us to look in subtle places for the sublime.

*

And if the search for sublime beauty requires travel to extreme places, so be it. We pull into Eureka Dunes after hours of bone-rattling unpaved washboard road. The steep voluptuous dunes, red and gold-tinged mountains, glistening light, the elemental spaciousness, floor me. Formed from debris scoured from an old lake bed and trapped by mountains, Eureka's dunes rise 700 feet above surrounding playa. Eureka's sands, densely packed and moisture laden, form steep, compact surfaces with only the crests of the tallest dunes soft and rumpled. These are "singing dunes;" movement down them sets off a ghostly baritone.

After dinner, I hike to a promontory 350 to 400 feet above camp. I revel in the remote strangeness, the dizzying expanse of sand and shadow as sun fades and stars flare. I lean gratefully into the cleansing wind and breathe deeply at the edge of a vastness I can scarcely grasp. For a moment, I am adrift in time, feeling the ancient waters lapping at the shores of the long disappeared lake, riding the wind carrying infinite particles of sand up these continually shape-shifting slopes, rising up from the tilt and thrust of continental plates grinding these mountains and valleys into creation.

All through our travels in Death Valley together, we engaged with the land, worked in oft harsh and unexpected conditions, and stood patiently in place to gaze through time. We cultivated stillness to see deeply, witnessed geological time writ subtly in stories in stone, tracked light and traced variations in color. We discerned environmental processes emerging like an intermittent river coming to surface. Maybe these kinds of lessons are implicit everywhere, but to find them yourselves, look closely at Greg and Janet's paintings. Better yet, get outside for an extended time to practice your own Death Valley seeing.

Rowland S. Russell received a PhD in Environmental Studies from Antioch University New England. A writer, editor and educator, he has a special interest in the American nature writing tradition and how it addresses the human-nature relationship. He has offered coursework in natural history, place-based writing, environmental literature, and ecopsychology. Since 2005 Rowland has been managing director of Whole Terrain, Journal of Reflective Environmental Practice. He has also co-founded or served on the board of a number of organizations at the crossroads of youth, nature, education and restoration, including King County World Conservation Corps, Seattle Youth Garden Works Monadnock Literary and Arts Festival, and the Glen Brook Writers Retreat.

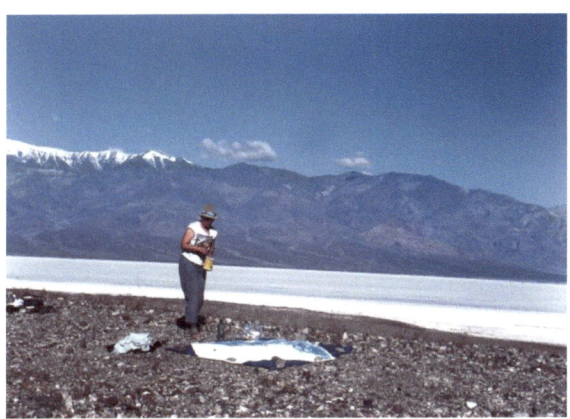

Making Art in Death Valley

In Death Valley everything - animal, mineral and vegetable, sky, water and earth – is in motion. Moved by earthquakes, footsteps, water, wind, wings, growth and upthrusts from deep in the earth. It is a grand, open, majestic land, with mountains and valleys and canyons and salt flats. It is also an intimate space, down to the tiny belly flowers, one eighth of an inch wide.

And that motion finds its way into my work. I have always painted from a kinesthetic, tactile and physical base. The spirit and movement animate me, and the force of things dictates my brush. After studying dance, my work gathered a greater perception of energy and movement – and in Death Valley the evidence of plate tectonics and weather systems and flash floods is an open book, the geology has no clothes, the earth is laid bare. There are truly transient things that change from hour to hour, day to day, and others that take thousands of years to move or wear down or build up. Then there is the sun and wind...

We as visitors are blessed to witness this intense and volatile place. The raven shows us the currents of the air, the morning tracks in the dunes show us the night life of lizard, bird and snake. Grand. Tiny. We find our place in between and among them all. Everything touches everything else – weather, rock, water, animal, human. Somehow we feel we are part of this power of movement and mass, like we are welcome here.

Janet Morgan, Death Valley National Park Artist-in-Residence, 2005, '06 and '08

Artwork of Death Valley

Badwater

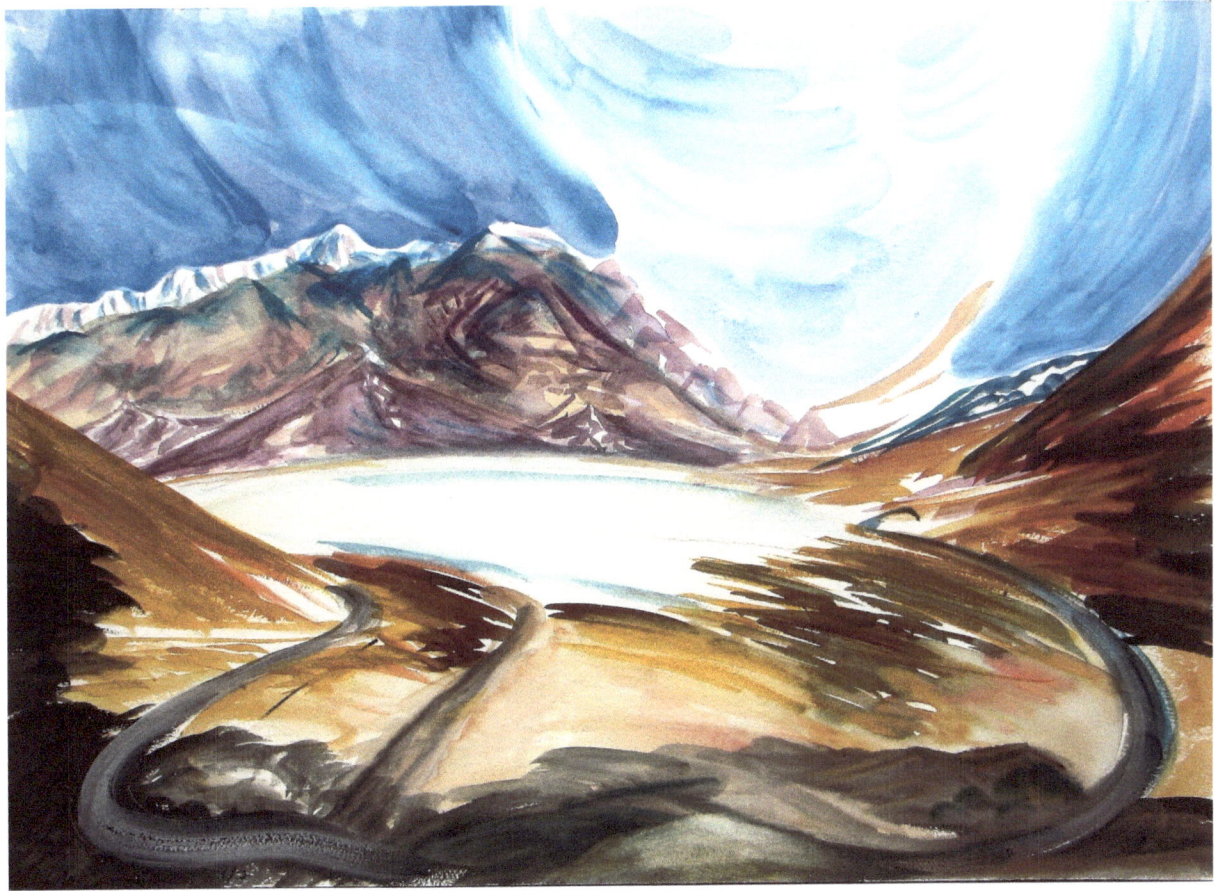

Badwater Shadows 2006 watercolor 14" x 20" Janet Morgan

Badwater from Aguereberry Point and the Hanaupah Canyon Fan

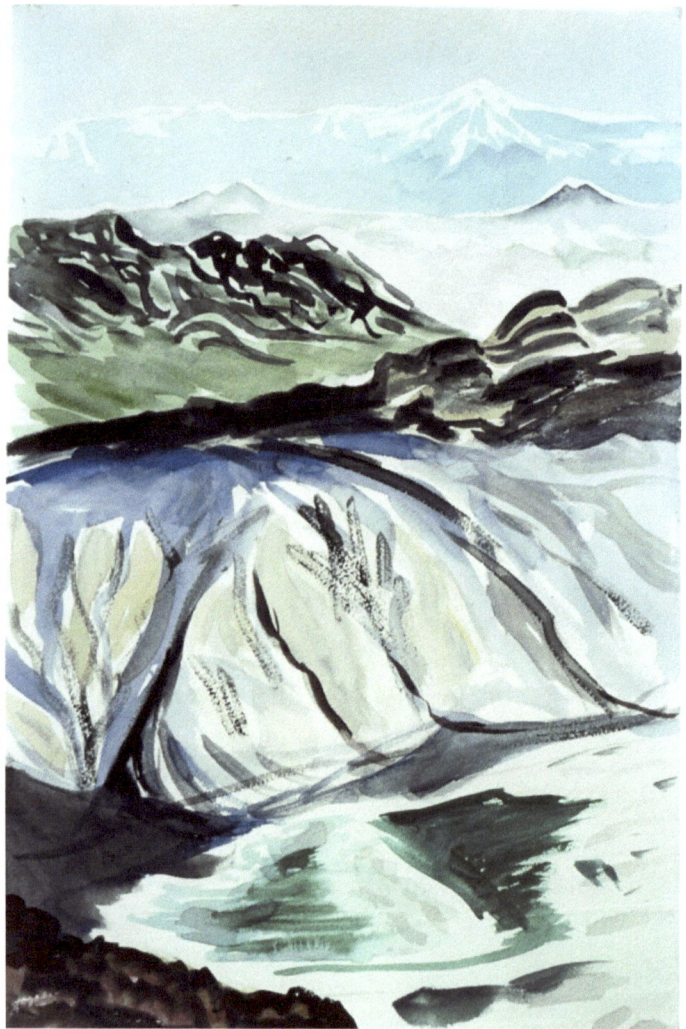

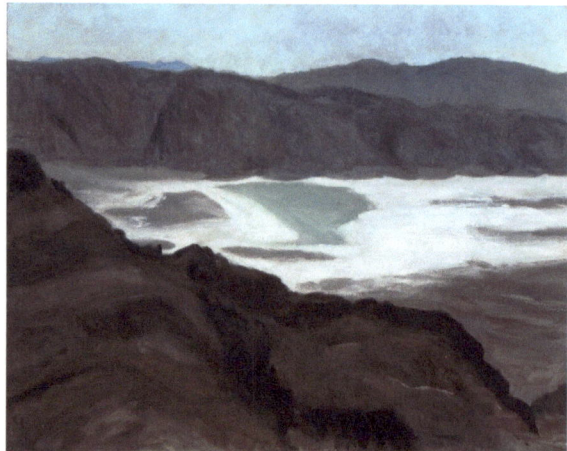

Aguereberry Point
2005 oil on panel 11" x 14"Gregory Frux

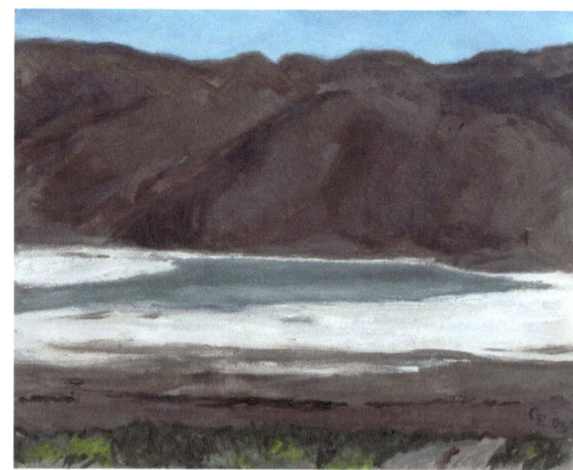

Aguereberry Point I 2005 watercolor 18" x 11" Janet Morgan

View from fan, Hanaupah Canyon
2005 o/p 8" x 10"Gregory Frux

Bridge Canyon

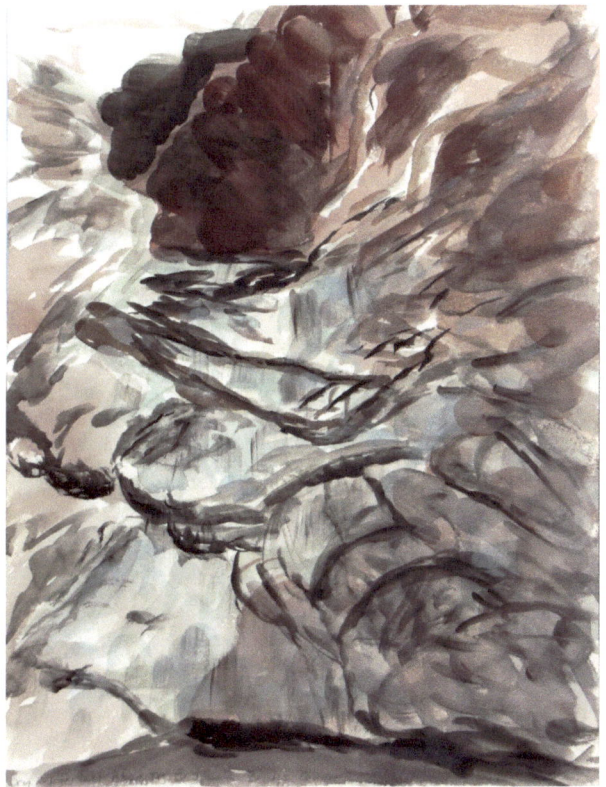

Bridge Canyon 2006 watercolor 12" x 9" Janet Morgan

Hanaupah Fan, Telescope Peak from Badwater

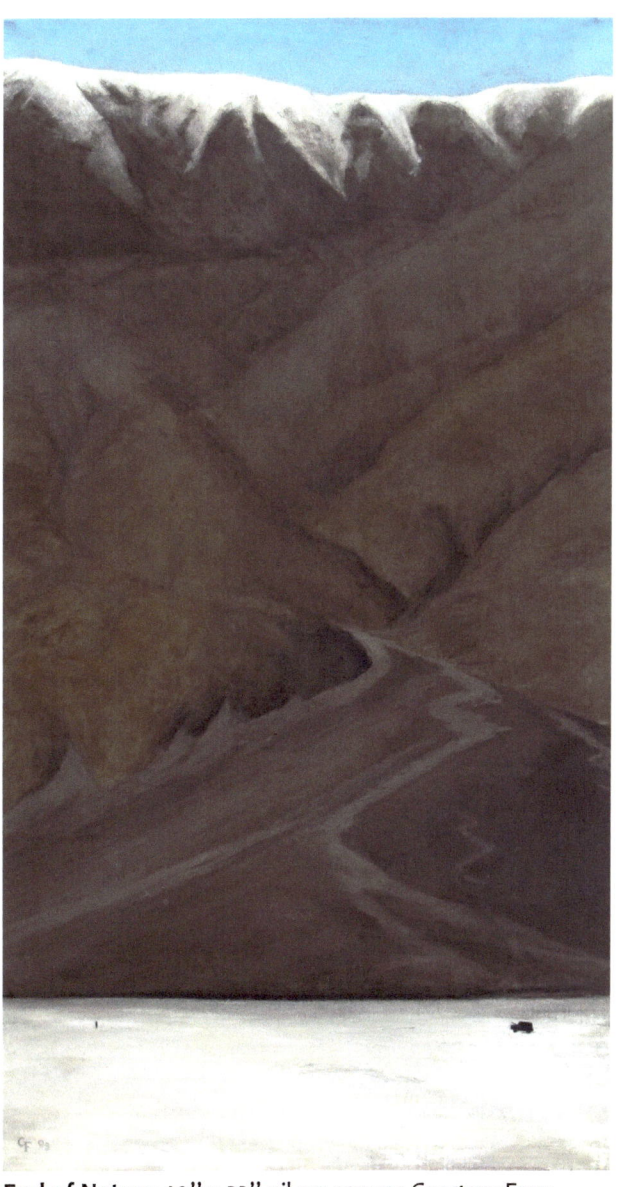

End of Nature 40" x 22" oil on canvas Gregory Frux

Corkscrew Peak

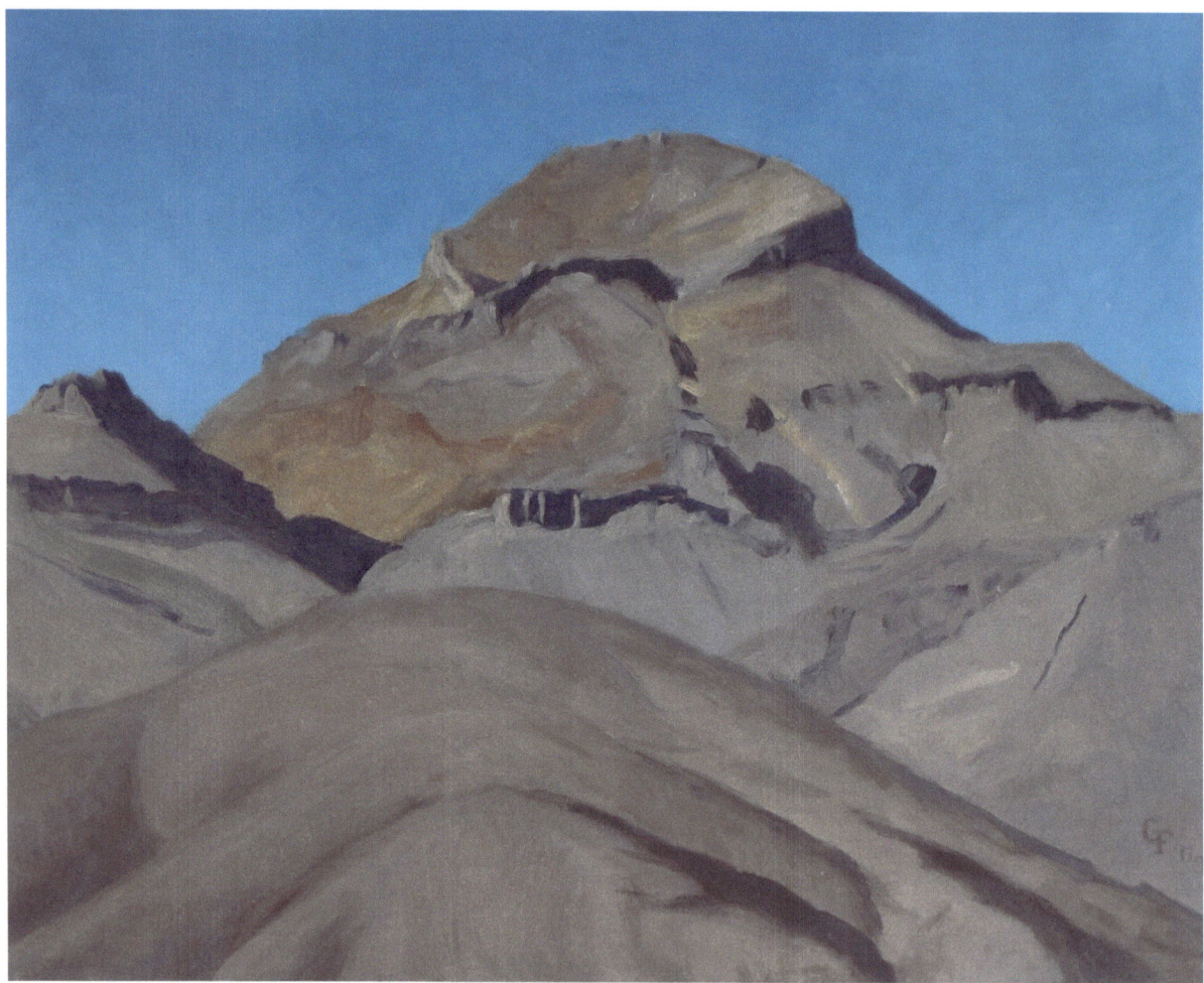

Corkscrew Peak 2009 oil on panel 11" x 14" Gregory Frux

Cottonwood Canyon

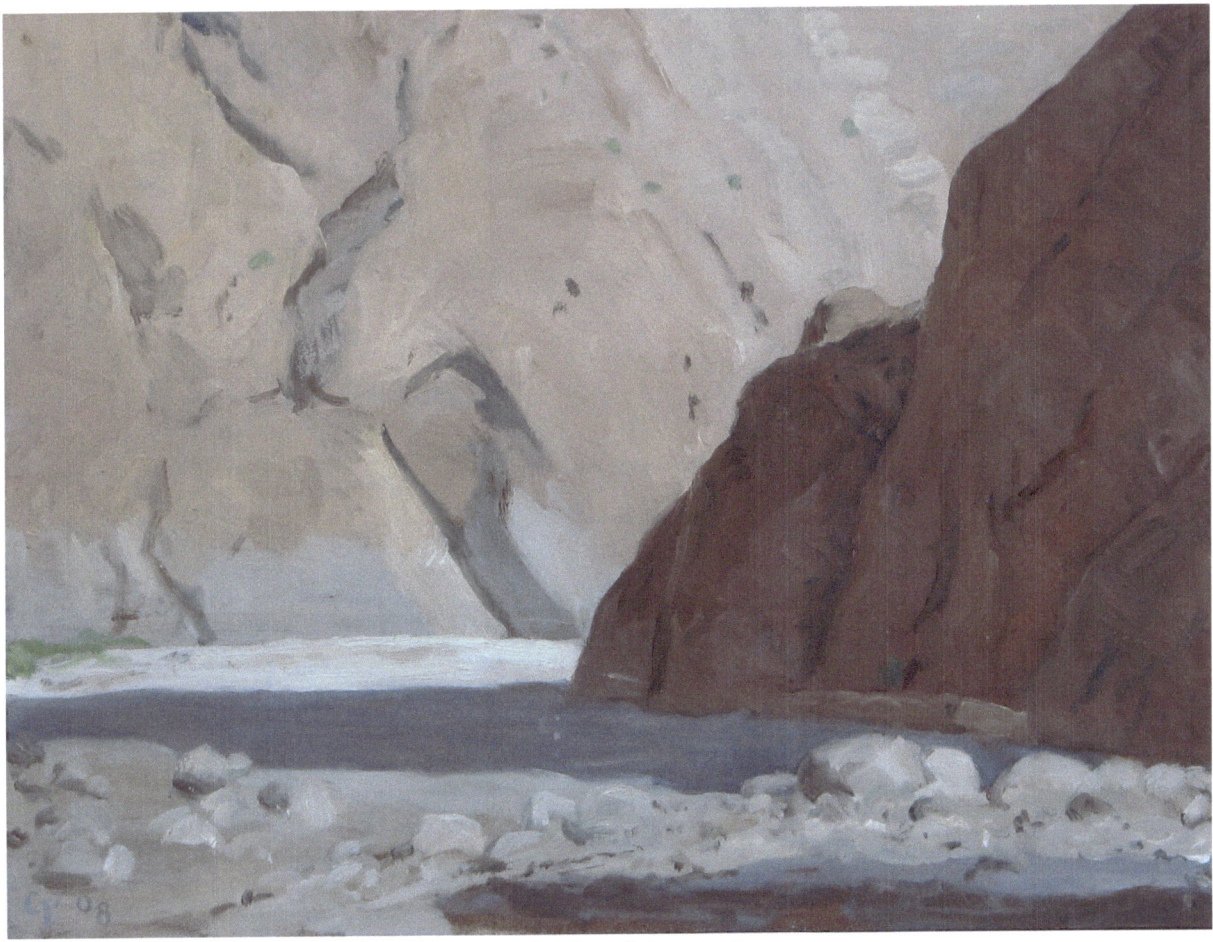

Narrows, Cottonwood Canyon 2008 oil on panel 9" x 12"Gregory Frux

Darwin Falls

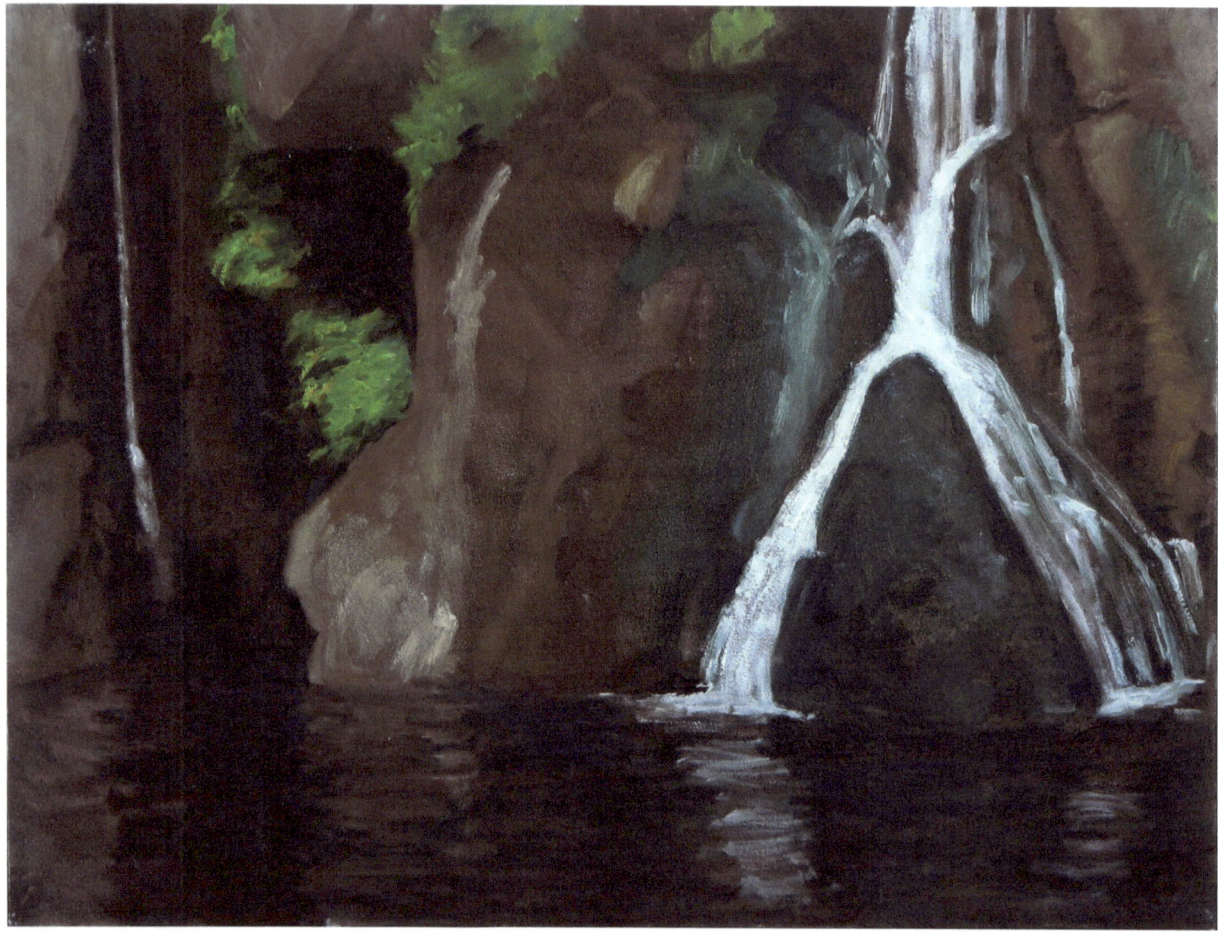

Darwin Falls 2005 oil on panel 9" x 12" Gregory Frux

Death Valley Buttes

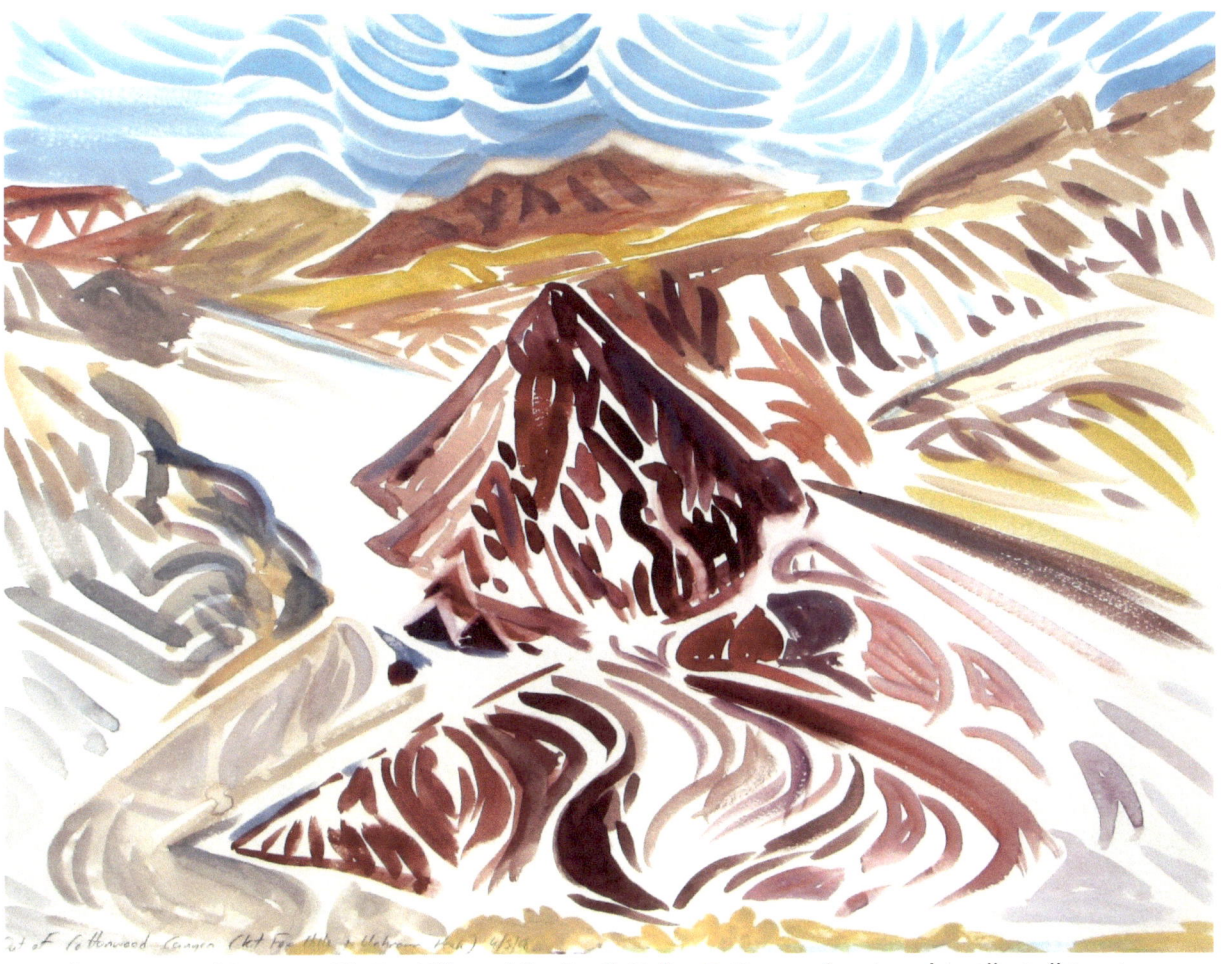

Out of Cottonwood Canyon – Kit Fox Hills and the Death Valley Buttes 2008 watercolor 15" x 20" Janet
Morgan

Death Valley Junction (park boundary)

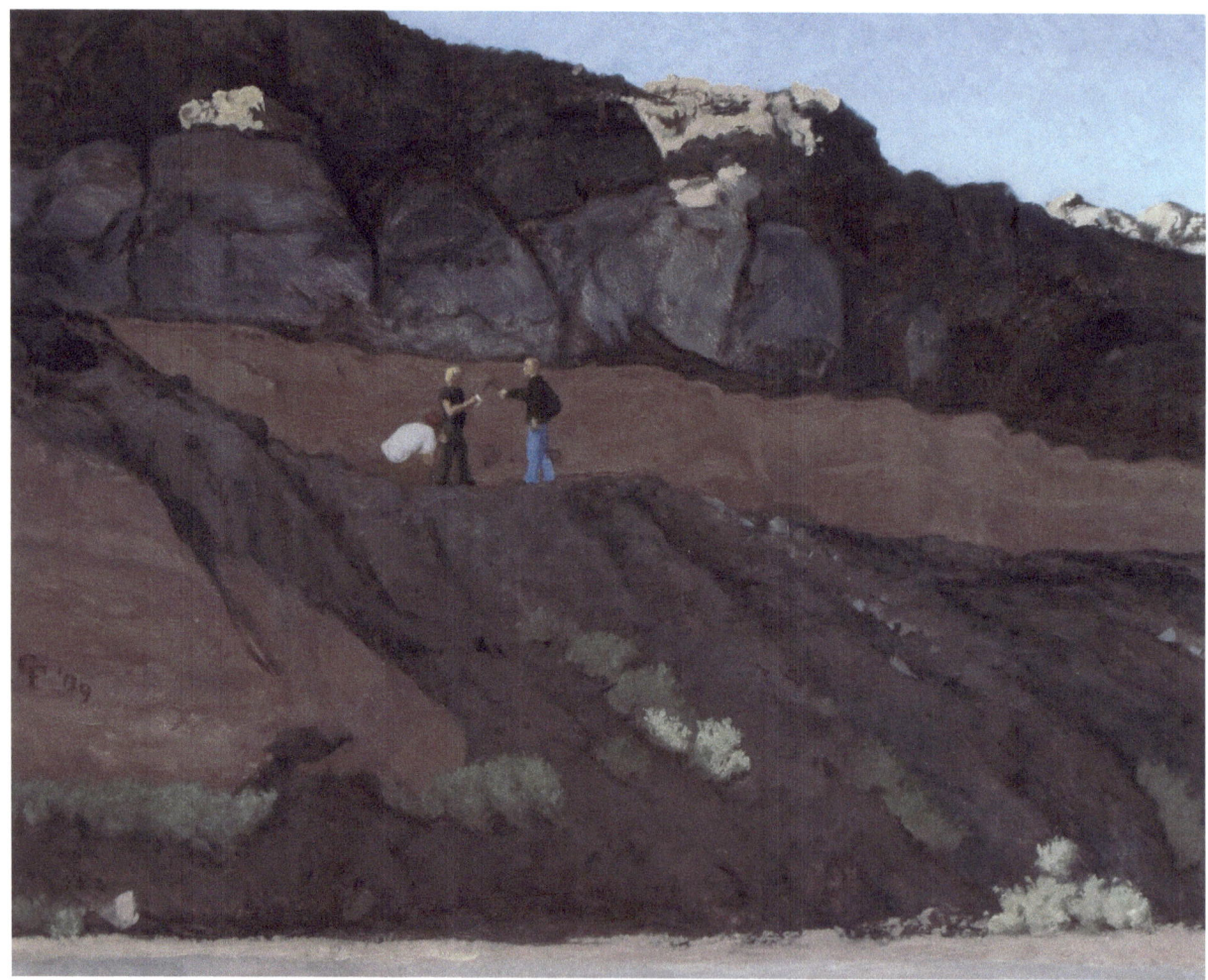

Road Cut, Death Valley 2009 oil on panel 11" x 14"Gregory Frux

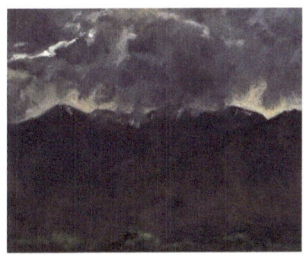

Storm over Panamints
2005 oil on panel 8" x 10"
Gregory Frux

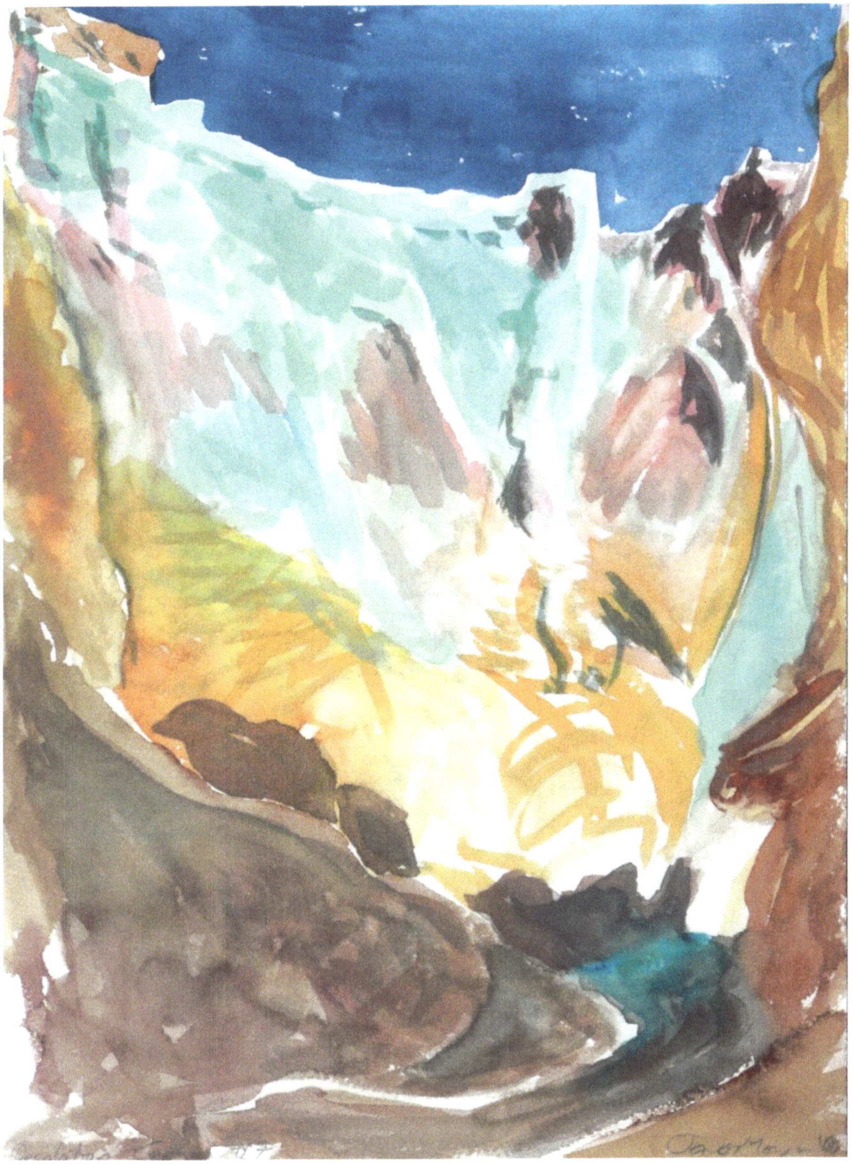

Desolation Canyon 2006 watercolor 12" x 9" Janet Morgan

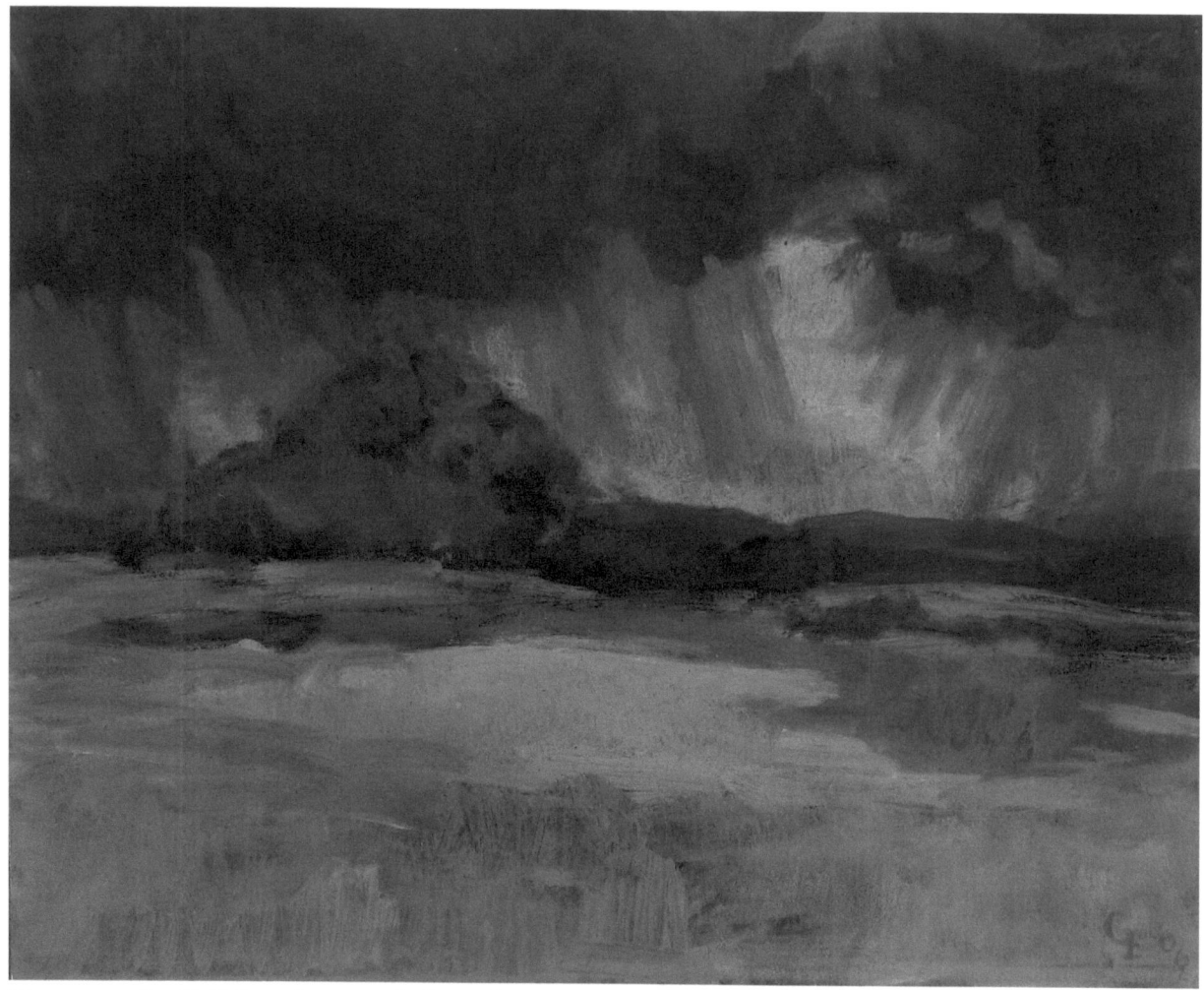

Storm over Death Valley oil on panel   8 x 10 Gregory Frux

Furnace Creek

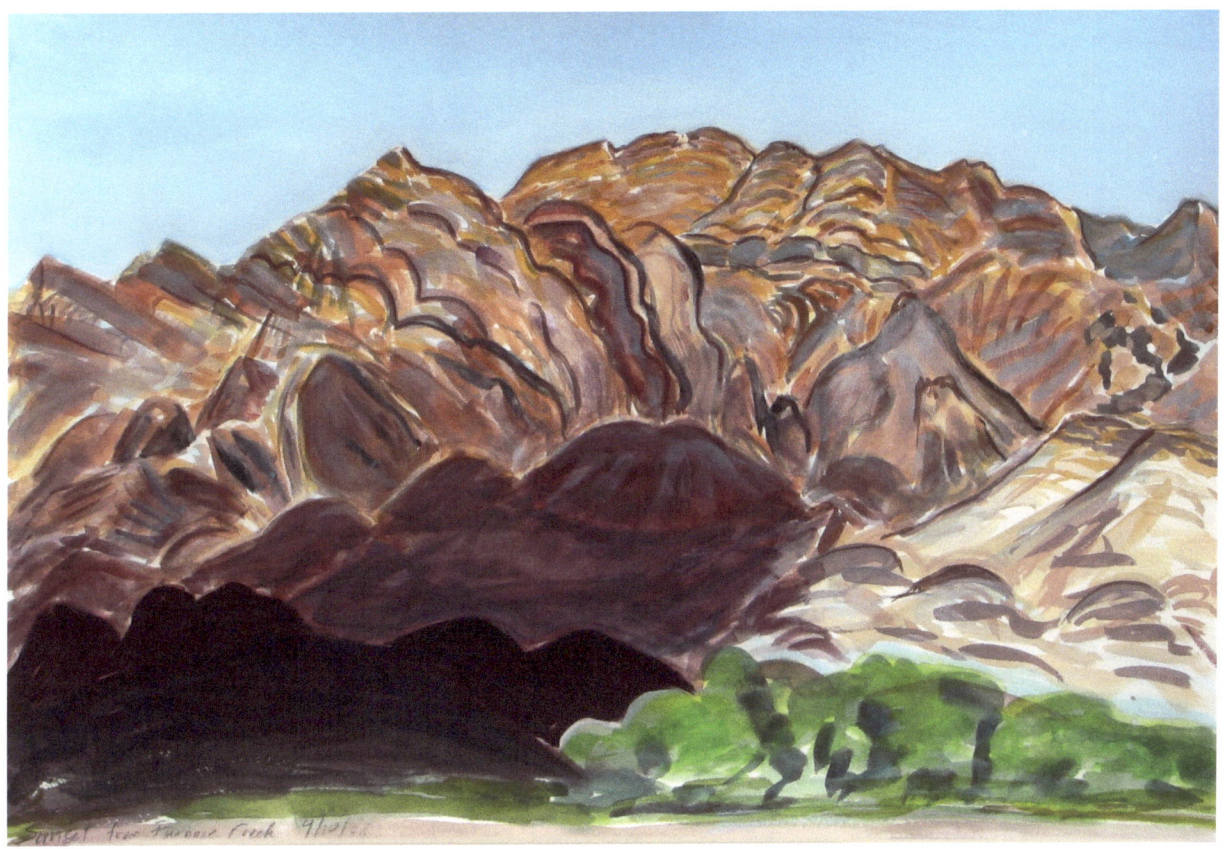

Sunset at Furnace Creek 2008 watercolor 14" x 20" Janet Morgan

Furnace Creek

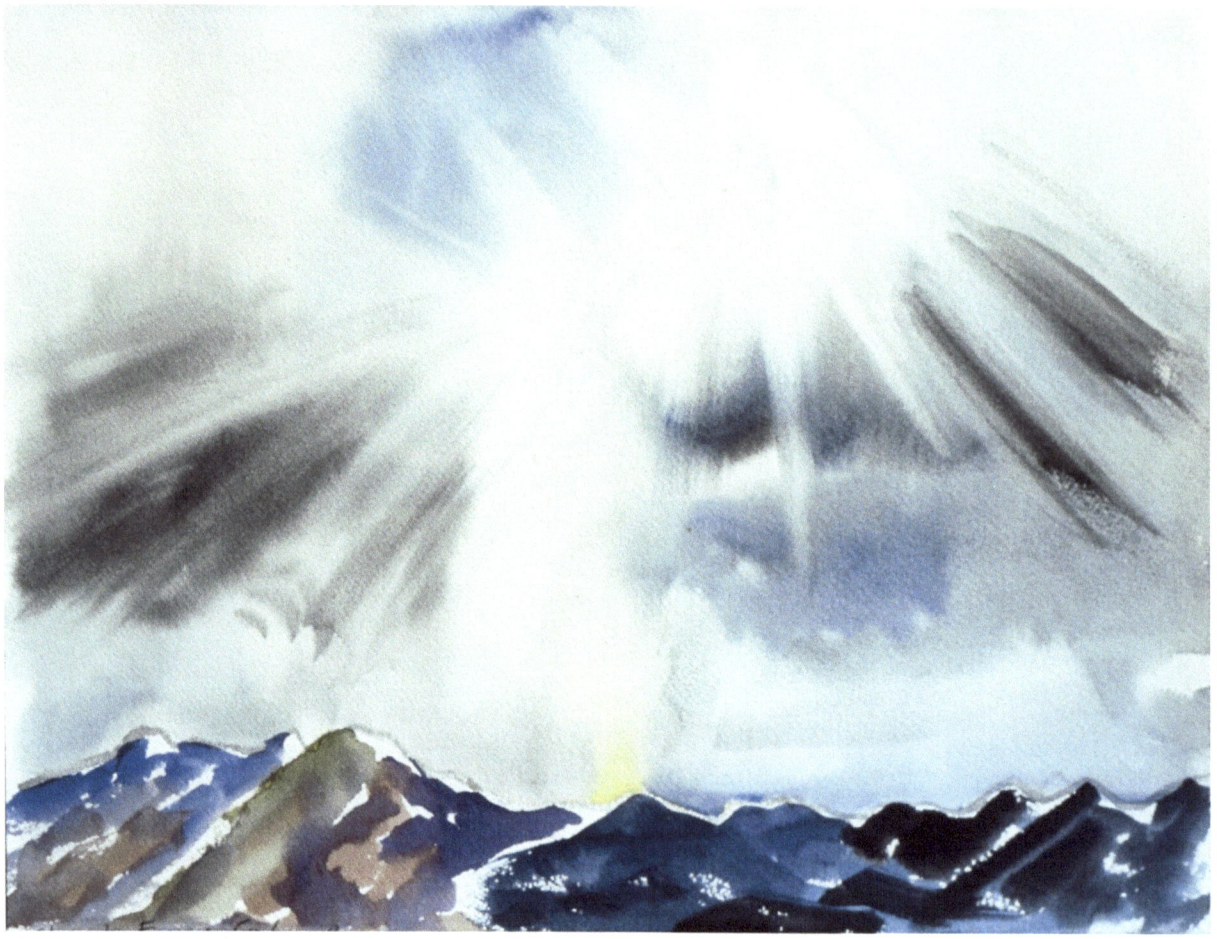

Sky at Furnace Creek I – Rays 2005 12" x 16" Janet Morgan

Golden Canyon

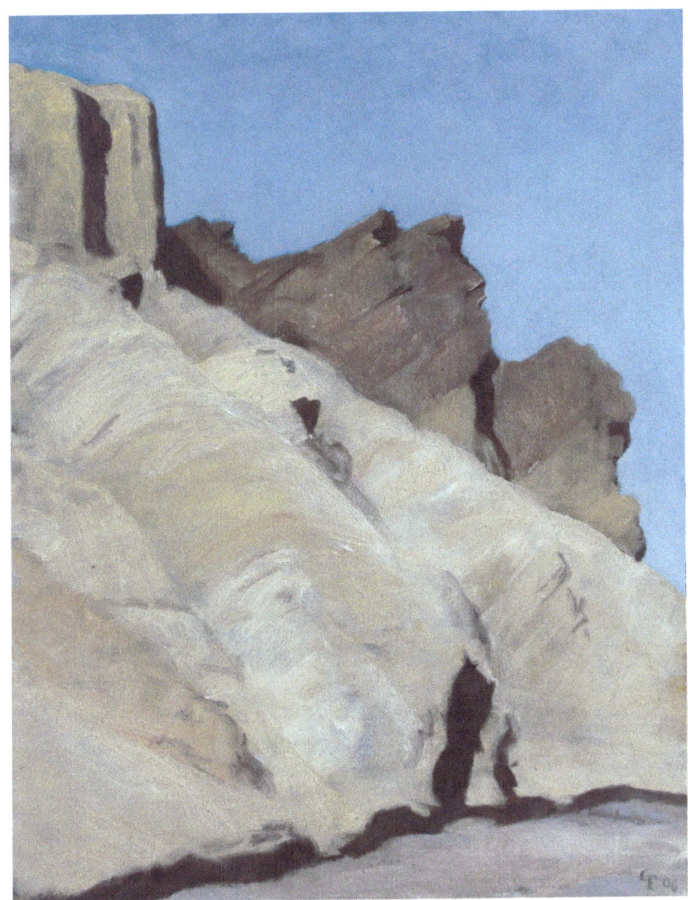

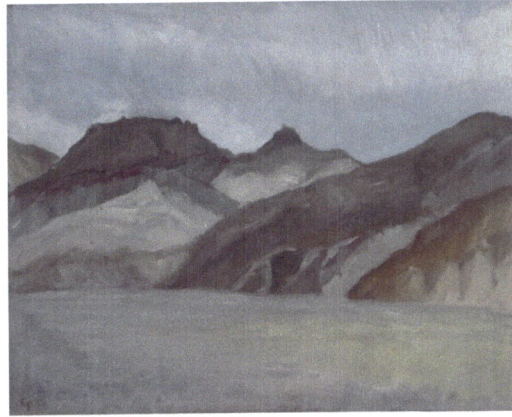

Badlands at Golden Canyon 2005 oil on panel 11" x 14"Gregory Frux

Golden Canyon I 2006 oil on panel 14" x 11"Gregory Frux

Golden Canyon

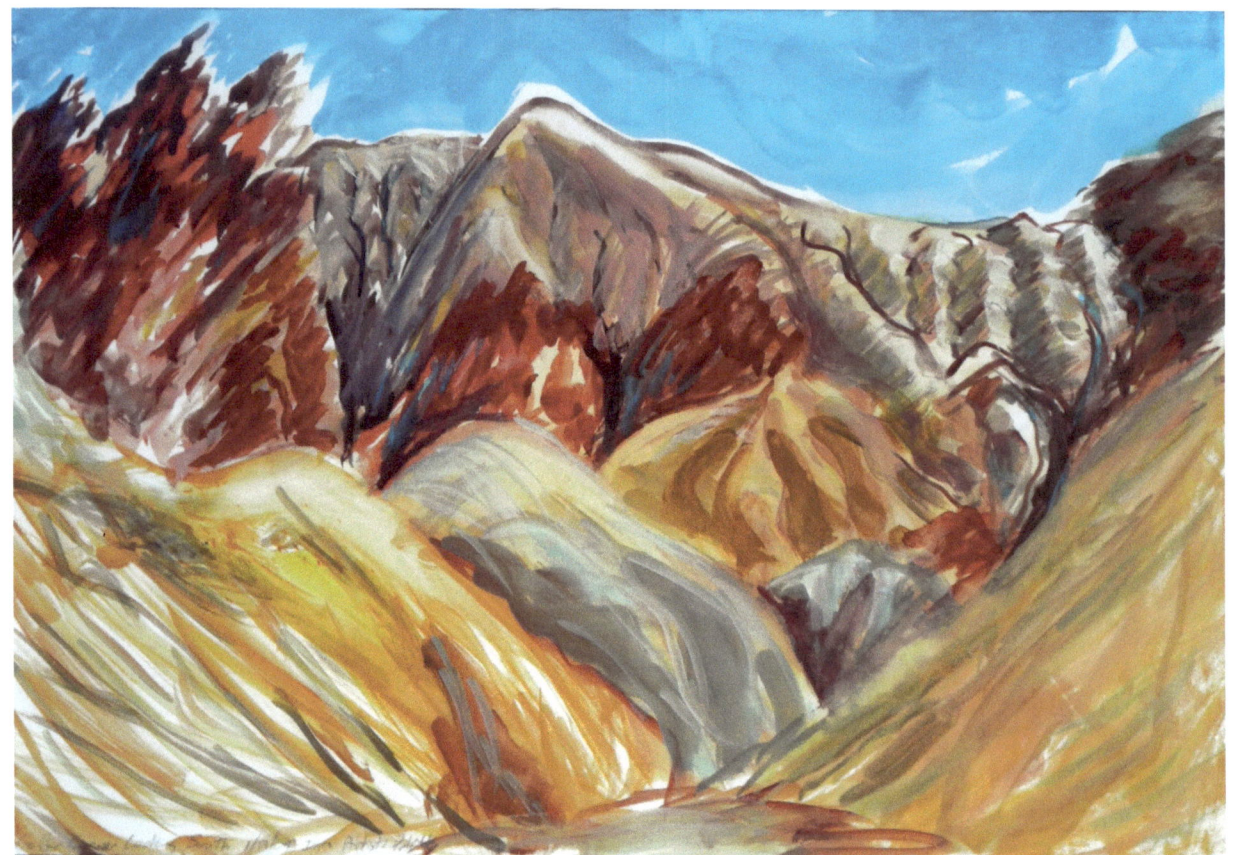

Golden Canyon Looking South Into Artist's Palette 2009 watercolor 12" x 18" Janet Morgan

Golden Canyon

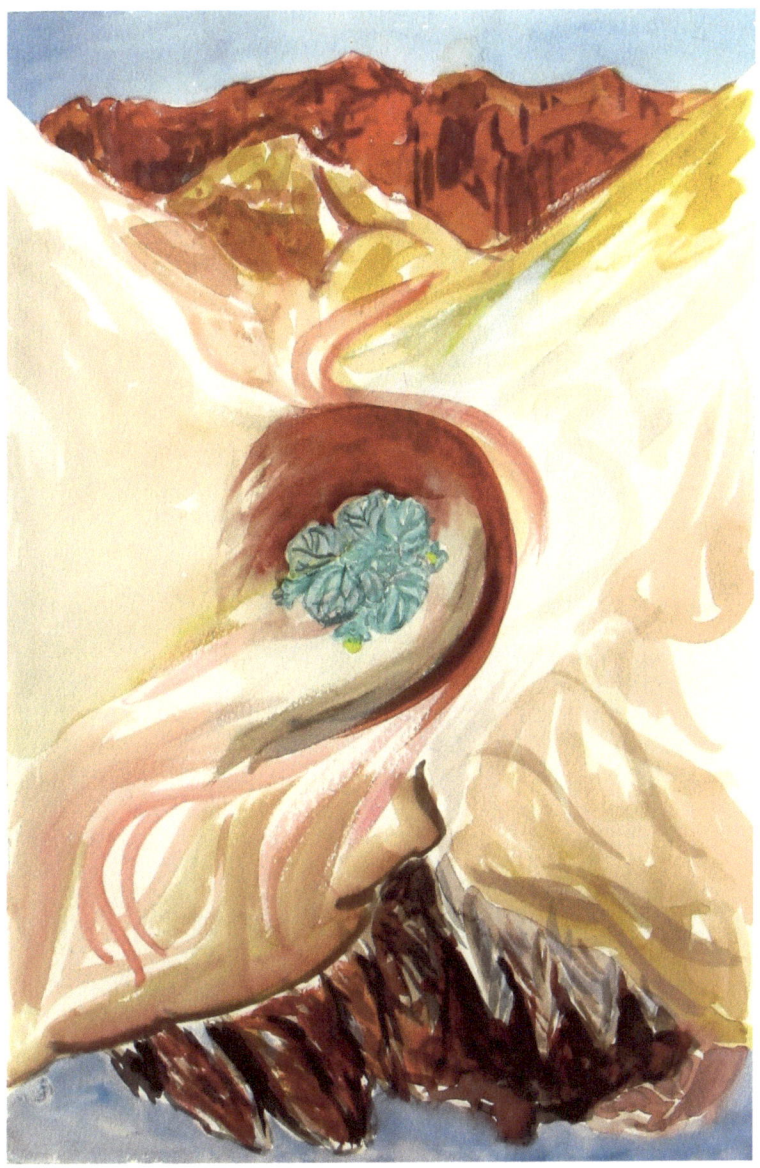

Up and Down in Golden Canyon 2005 watercolor 12 x 18"J

Golden Canyon

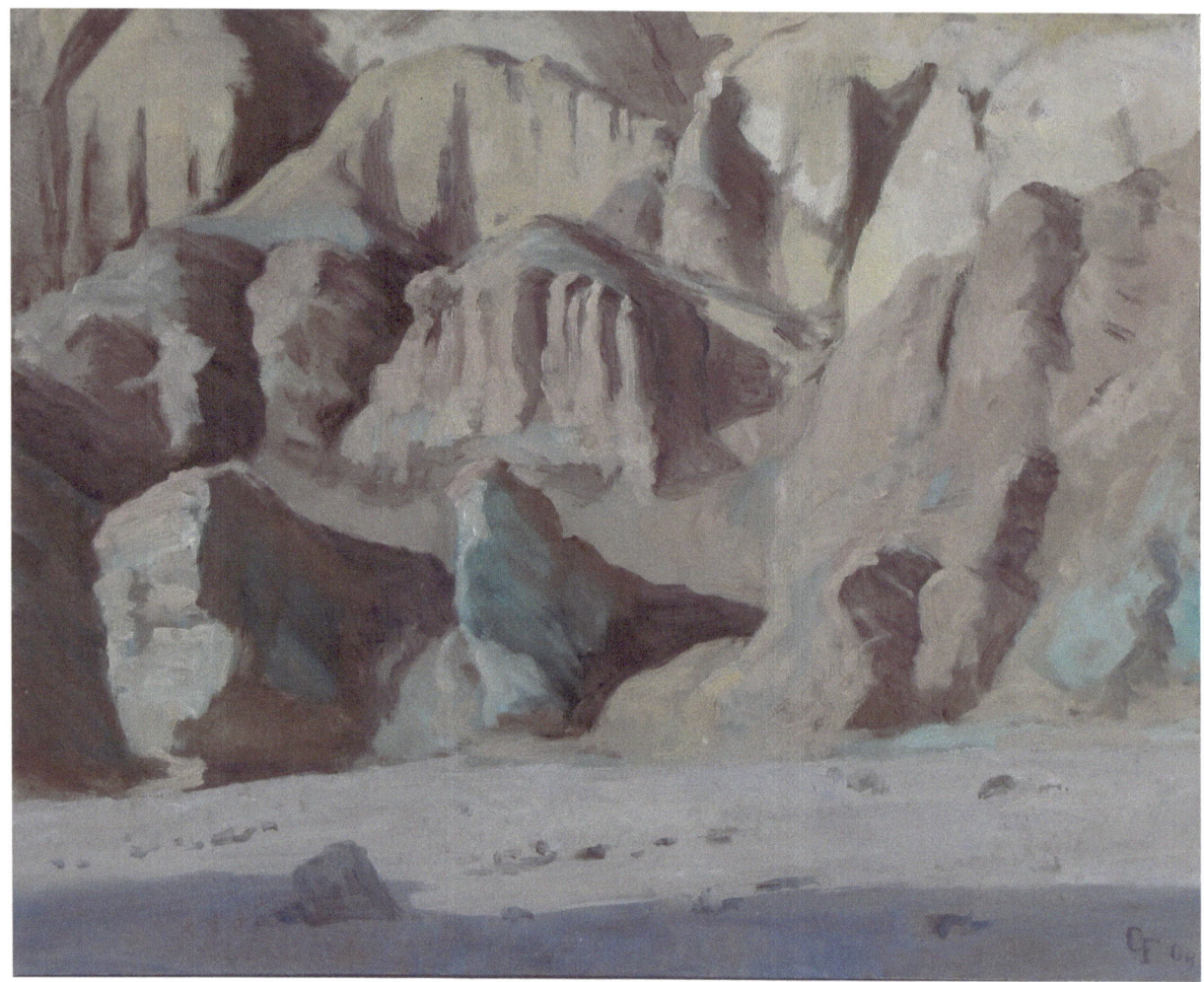

Golden Canyon 11" x 14" oil on panel Gregory Frux

Gower Gulch

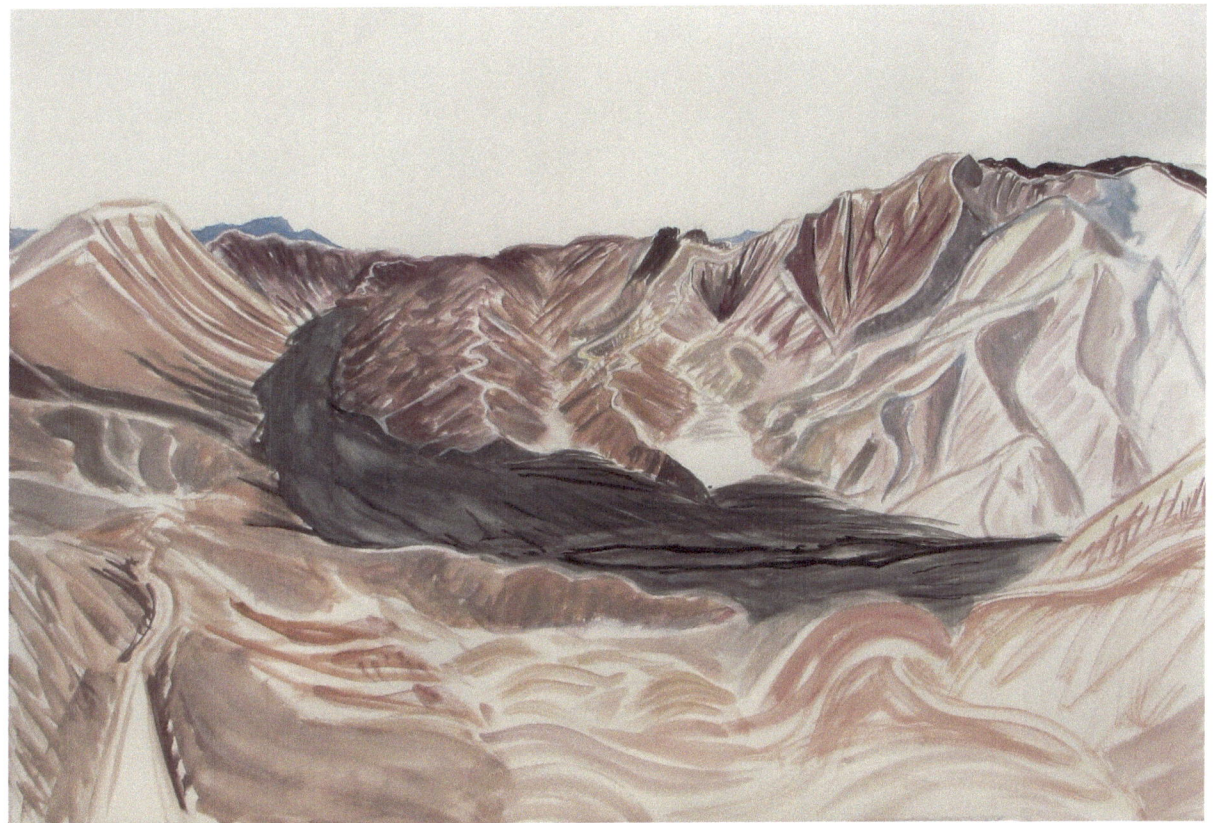

Gower Gulch 2009 watercolor 26" x 40" Janet Morgan

Last Chance Mountains

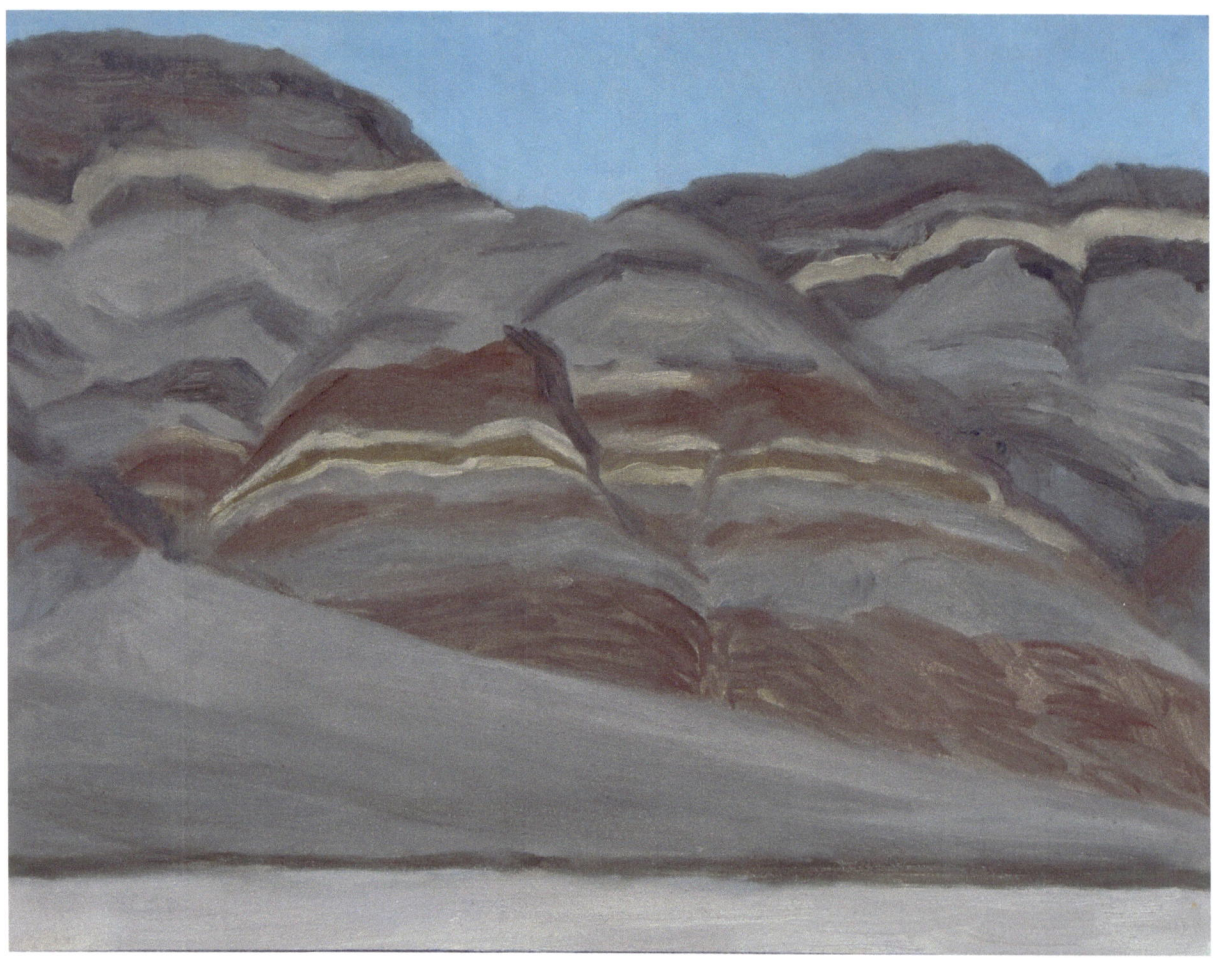

Last Chance Mountains 2008 oil on panel 9" x 12" Gregory Frux

Mosaic Canyon

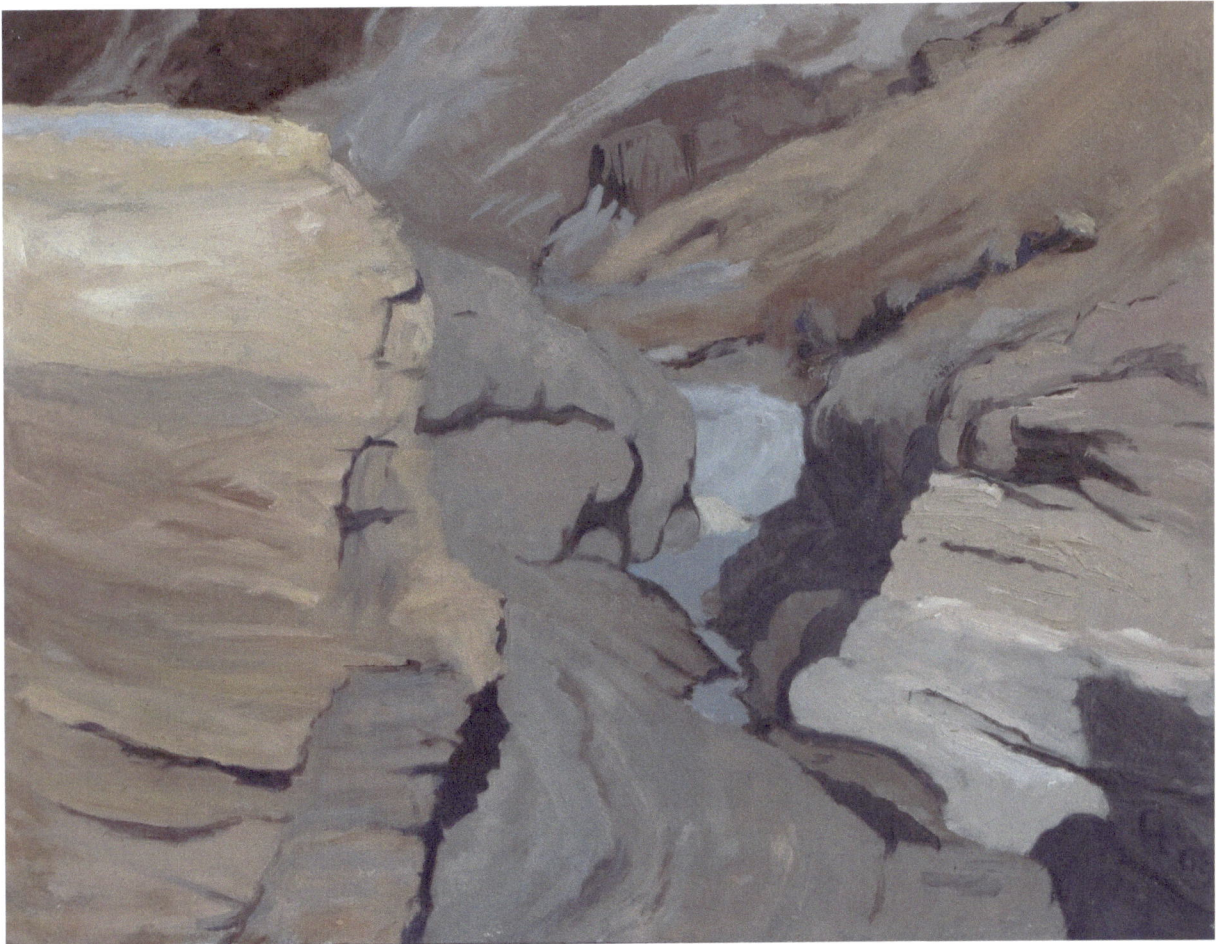

Mosaic Canyon 2009 9" x 12" oil on panel Gregory Frux

Mosaic Canyon and Mustard Canyon

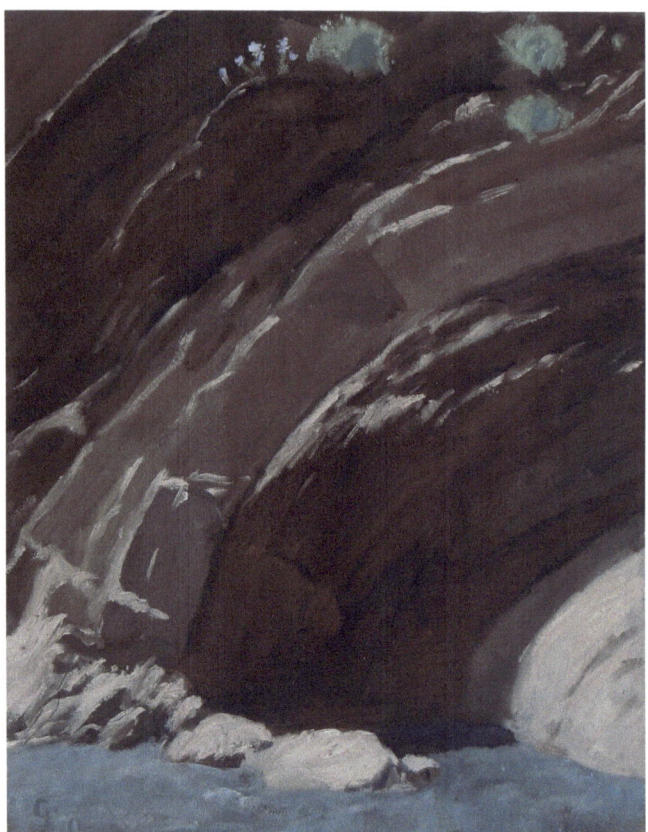

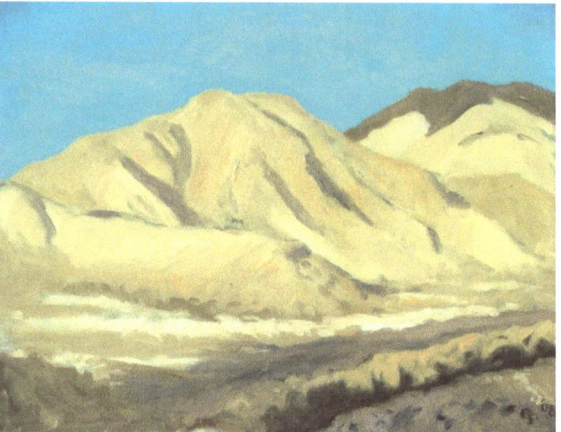

Mustard Canyon 2008 oil   9" x 12" Gregory Frux

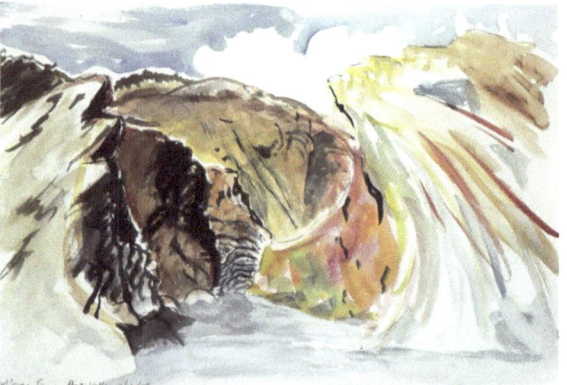

Mosaic Canyon 2006 watercolor 12" x 18" Janet Morgan

Mosaic Canyon, 9" x 12" oil on panel Gregory Frux

Panamint Valley

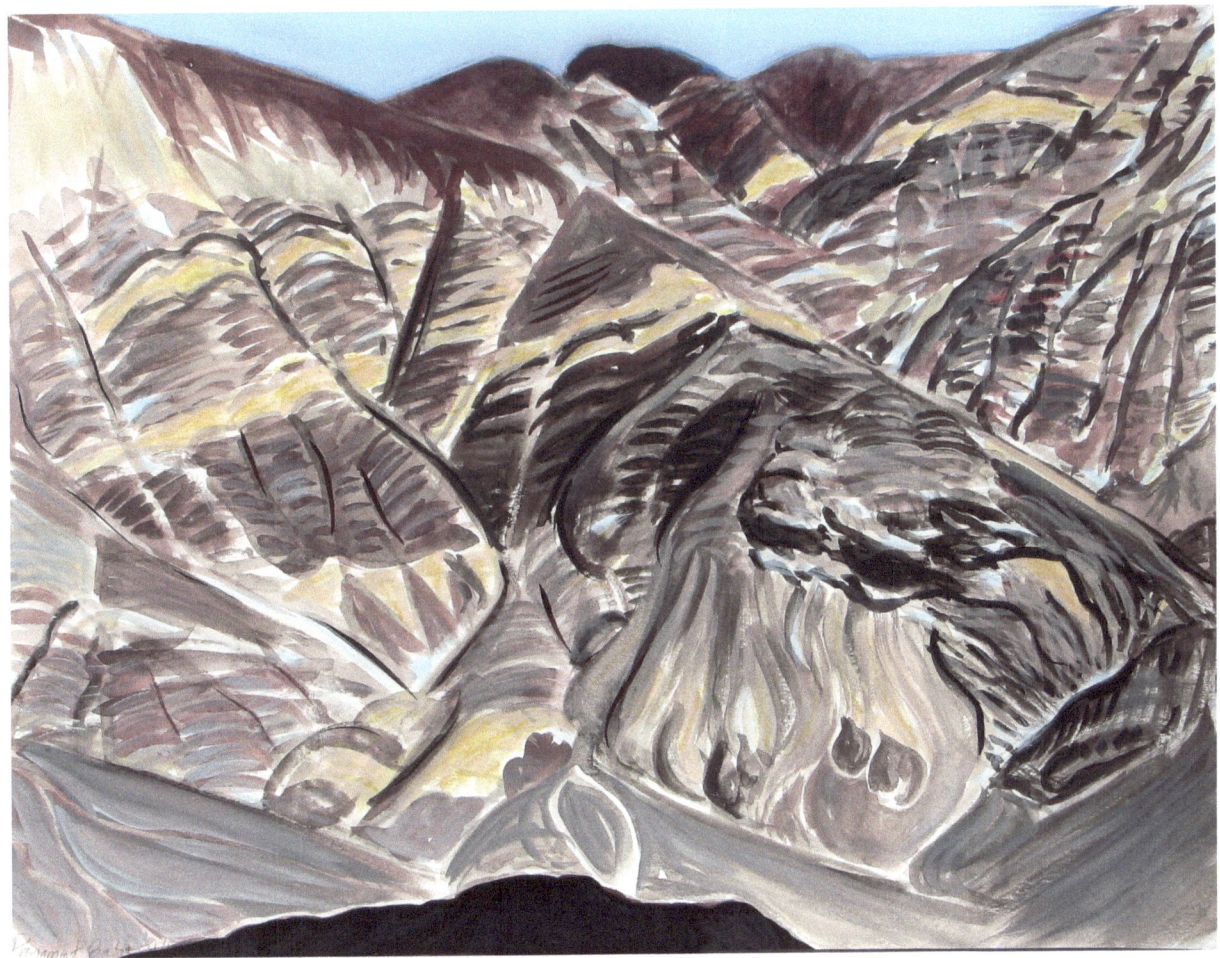

Panamint Butte 2008 watercolor 15" x 20" Janet Morgan

Panamint Valley

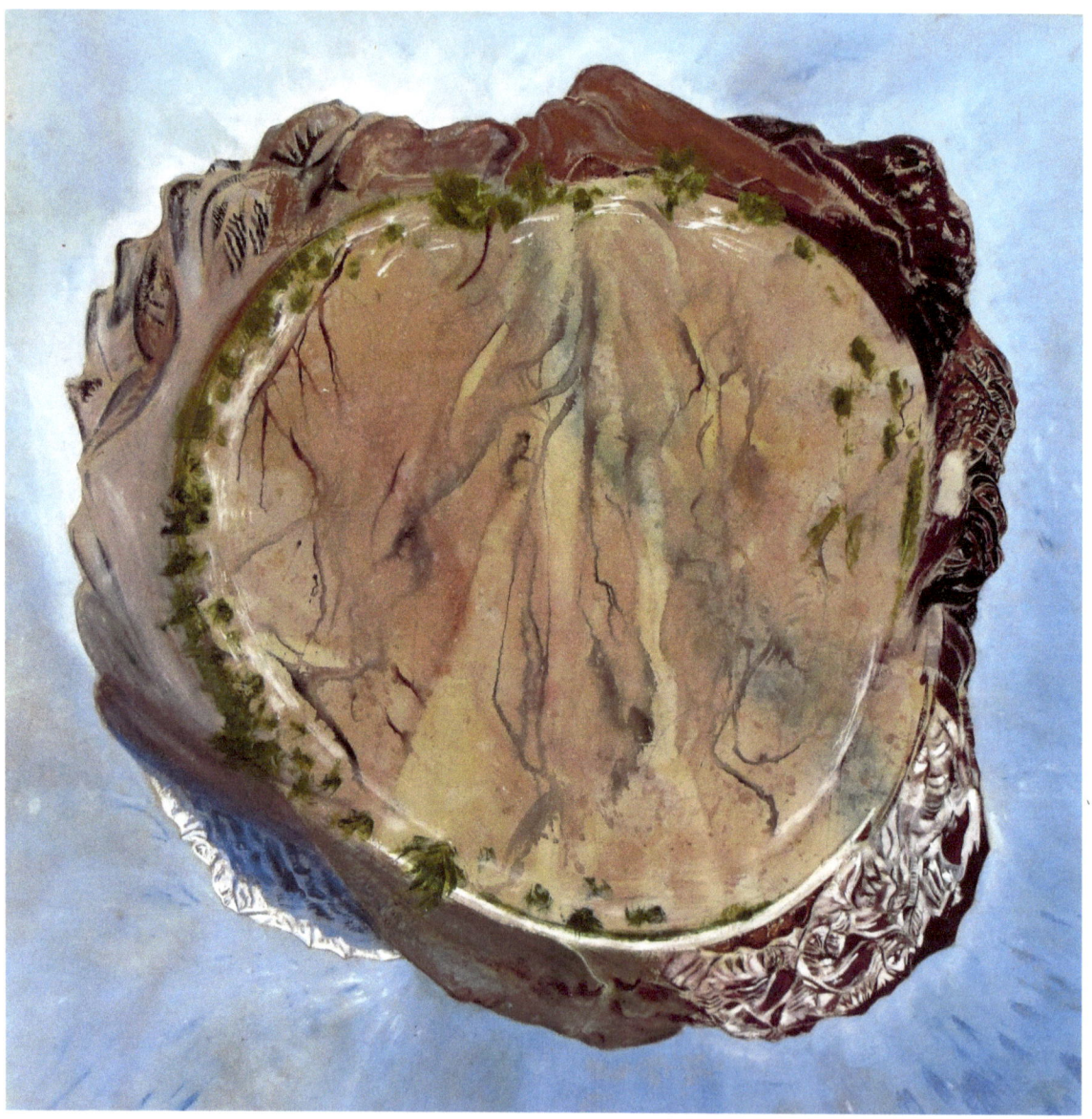

Looking Down on Panamint Valley 2007 Acrylic on muslin, 54" x 54" Janet Morgan In Janet's Book

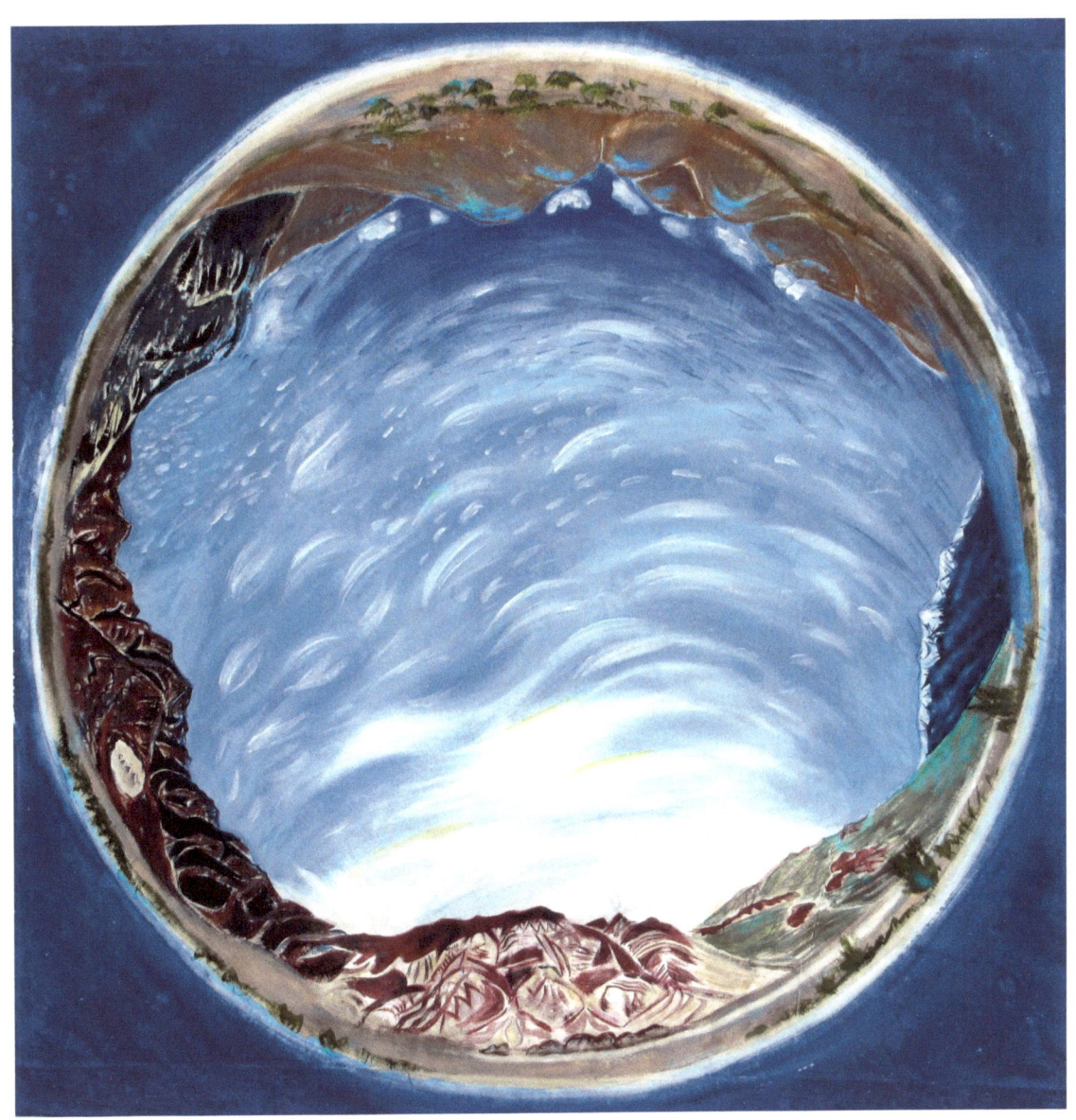

Looking Up in Panamint Valley 2007 Acrylic on muslin, 54" x 54" Janet Morgan

Saline Valley

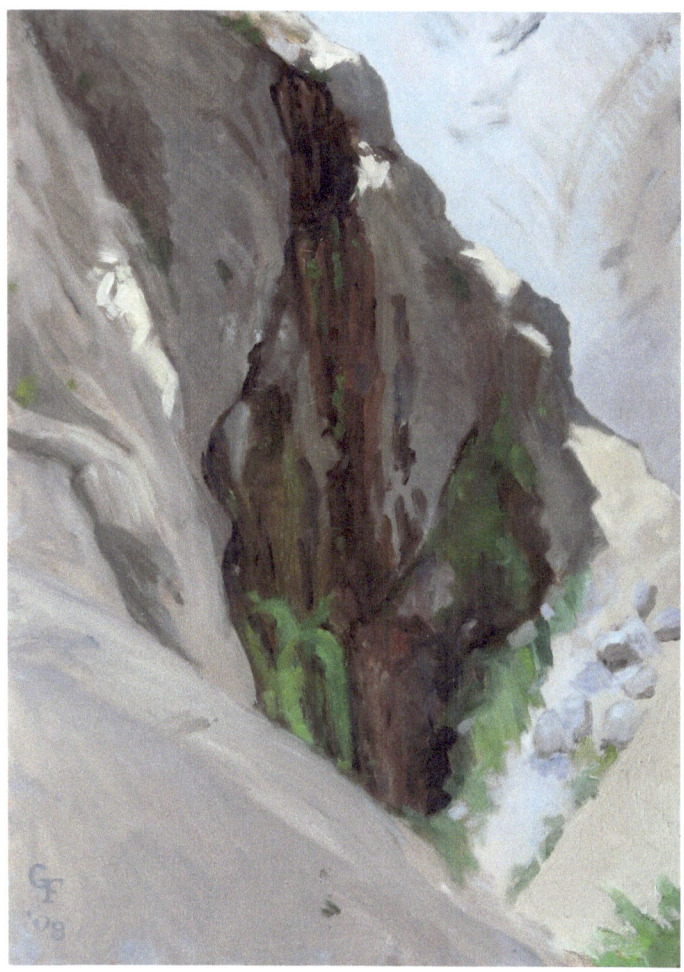

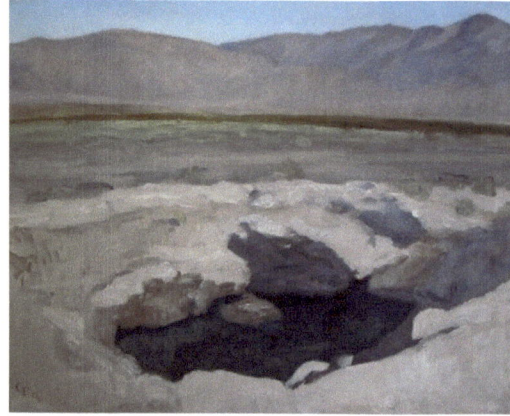

Hot Spring Saline Valley 2006 o/p 11" x 14" Gregory Frux

McElvoy Seep 2008 oil on panel -12" x 9" Gregory Frux-

Saline Valley, Surprise and Titus

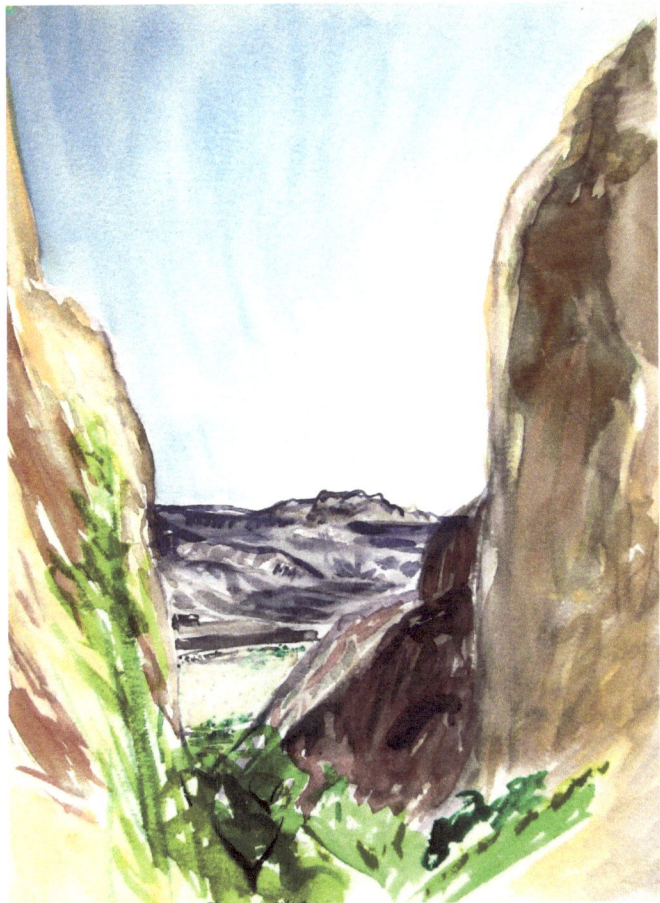

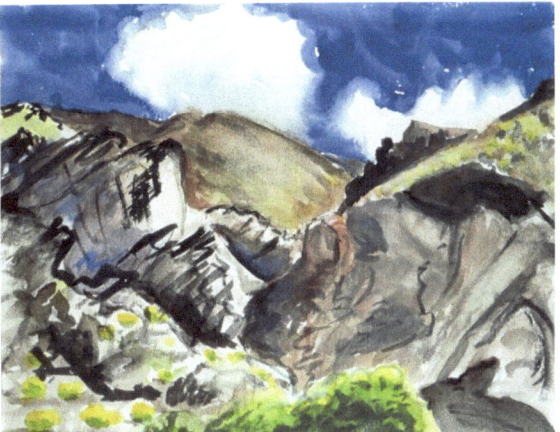

Surprise Canyon Up 2005 watercolor 9" x 12"
Janet Morgan

Titus Canyon

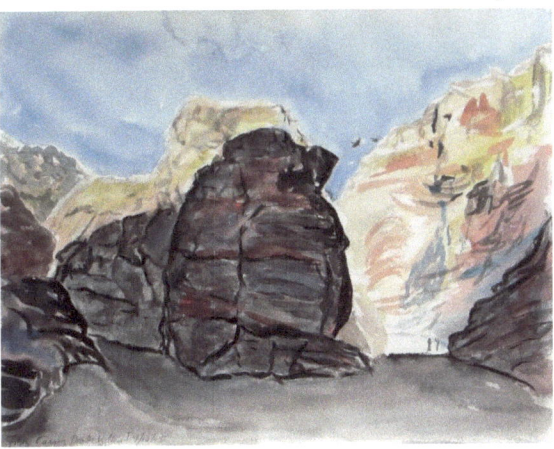

Looking out McElvoy Canyon 2006 watercolor 12" x 9"
Janet Morgan

Titus Canyon I 2005 watercolor 12" x 16" Janet
Morgan

Surprise Canyon

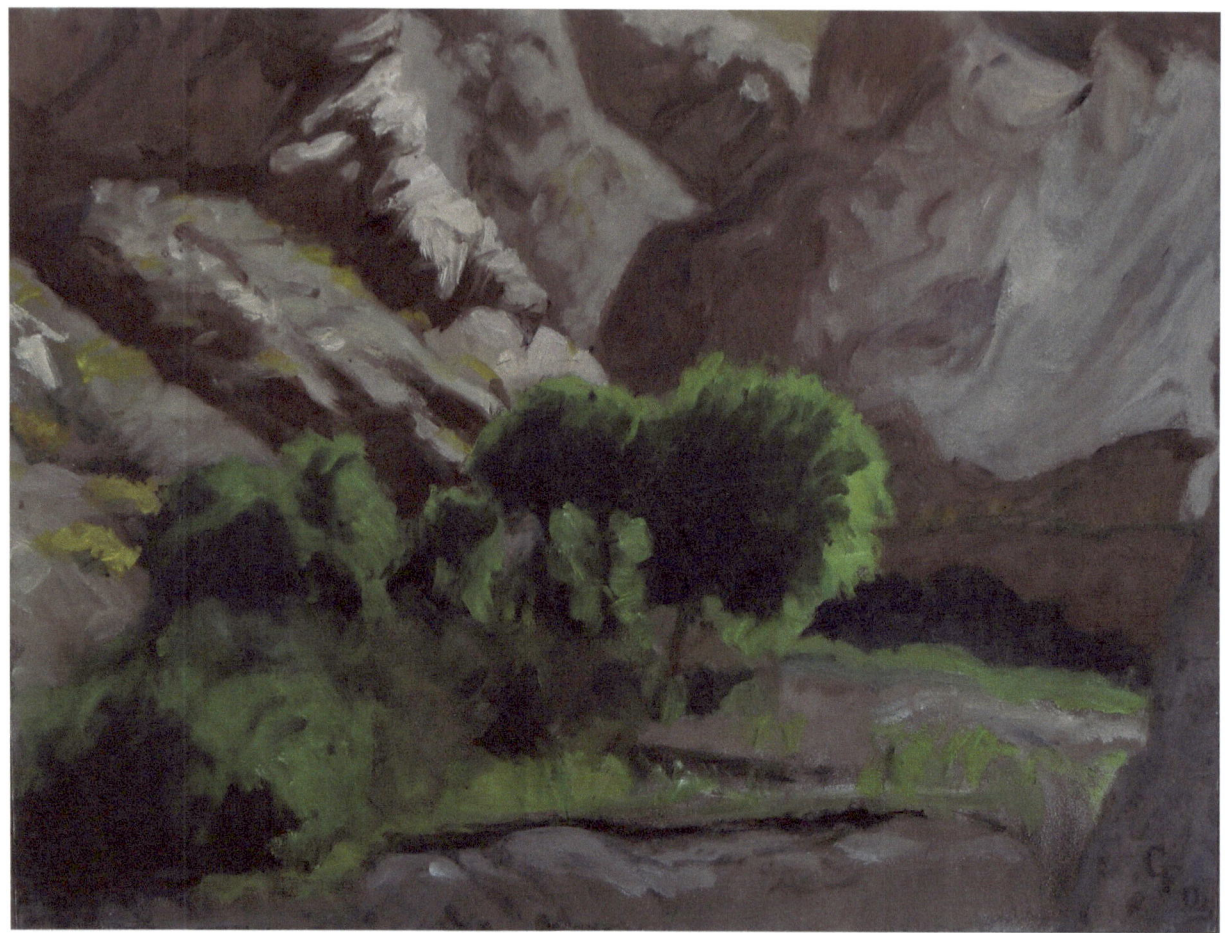

Surprise Canyon, West View 2005 oil on panel 9" x 12" Gregory Frux

Ubehebe Crater

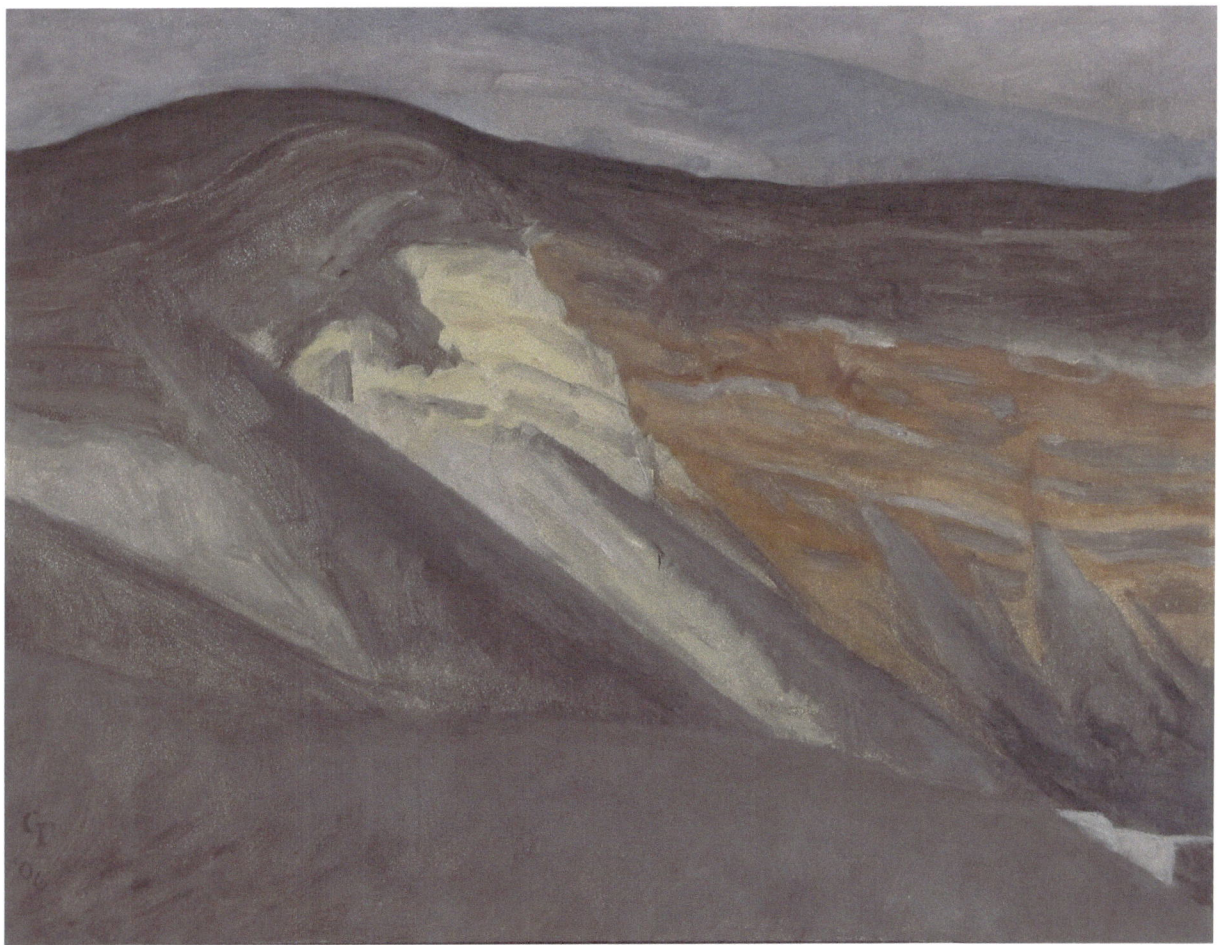

Crater 2006 oil on panel 12" x 16" Gregory Frux

Ubehebe Crater

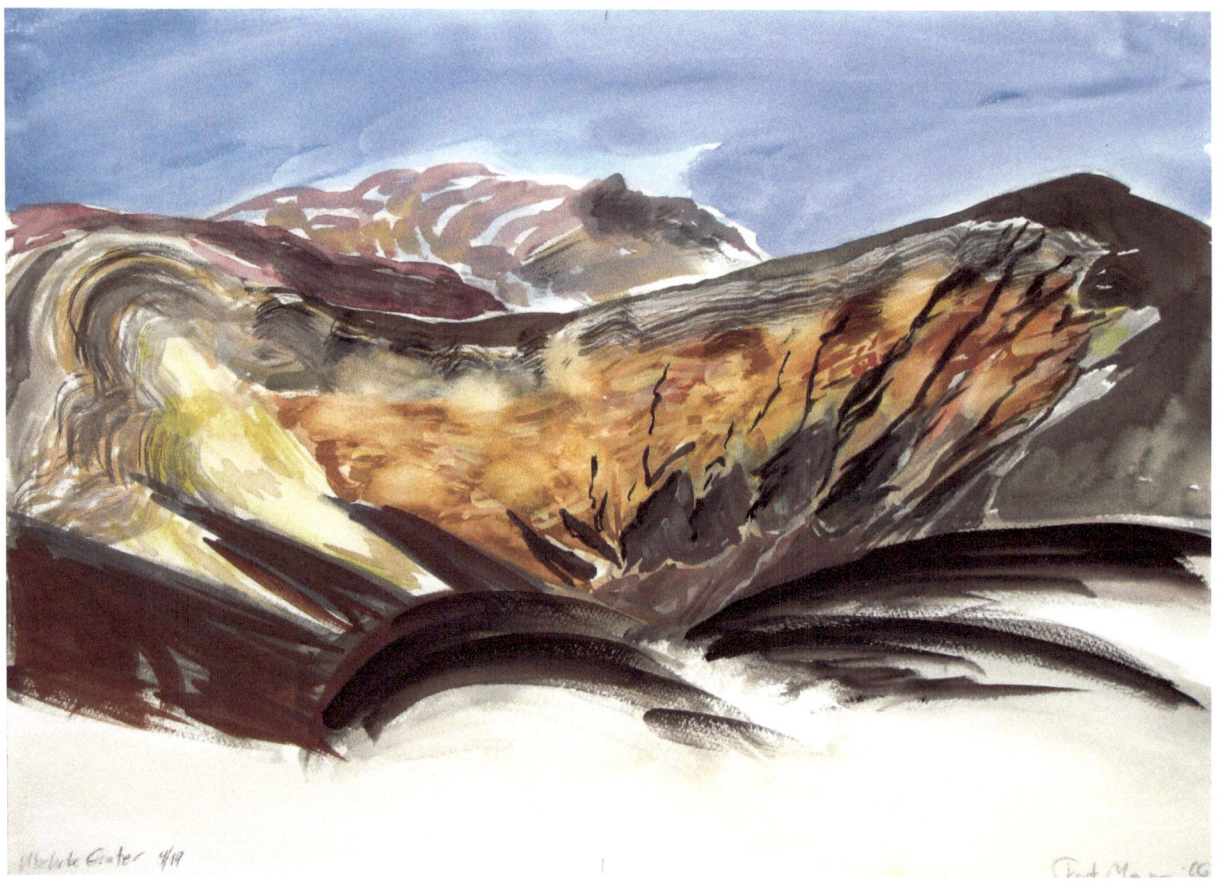

Ubehebe Crater 2006 watercolor 14" x 20" Janet Morgan

Zabriskie Point

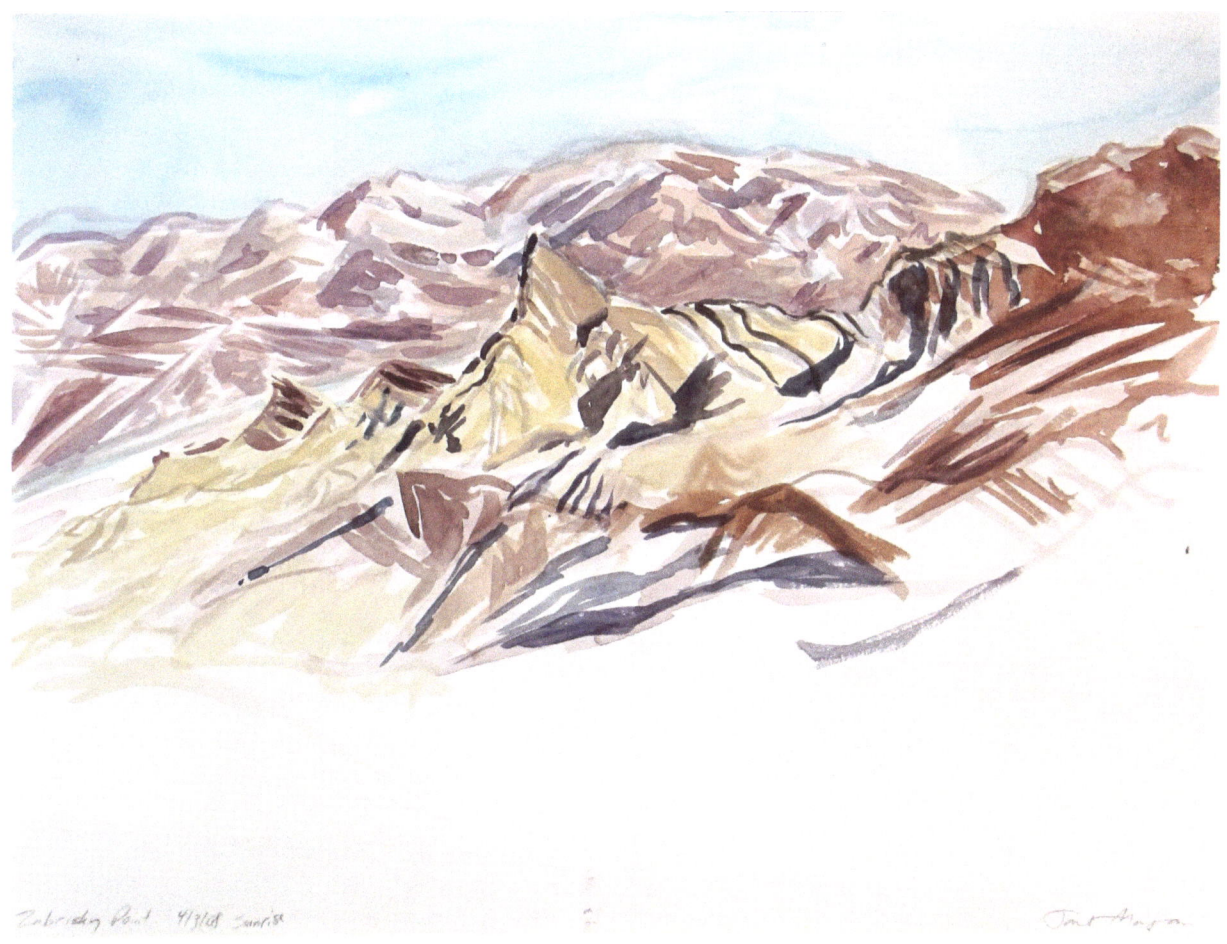

Zabriskie Point 4/9/08 Sunrise

Zabriskie Point Sunrise 2008 watercolor 15" x 20" Janet Morgan

Janet Morgan has explored Death Valley five times, including three times as the Death Valley National Park Artist-in-Residence. She has endured hailstorms, windstorms and sandstorms, soaked in hot springs as bats dove in for a drink, crossed the Last Chance Mountains, painted on the salt flats 280 feet below sea level and visited with ravens everywhere. She has worked with grade school students in the Death Valley R.O.C.K.S. Program, given ranger talks and taught drawing for a university geology field school. Her children's book *Welcome to Death Valley* was created from the artwork done during these visits and is available on her websites.

Janet has had a long and varied creative life, painting all over the world, illustrating books, making celebration art and teaching to people of all ages. She has been artist-in-residence at the Weir Farm National Historic Site in Connecticut, the Babayan Culture House in Turkey and the Omega Institute in Rhinebeck New York. In addition to Death Valley, she has created art in the American Southwest, the Rockies, the high Andes, Kyrgyzstan and Antarctica.

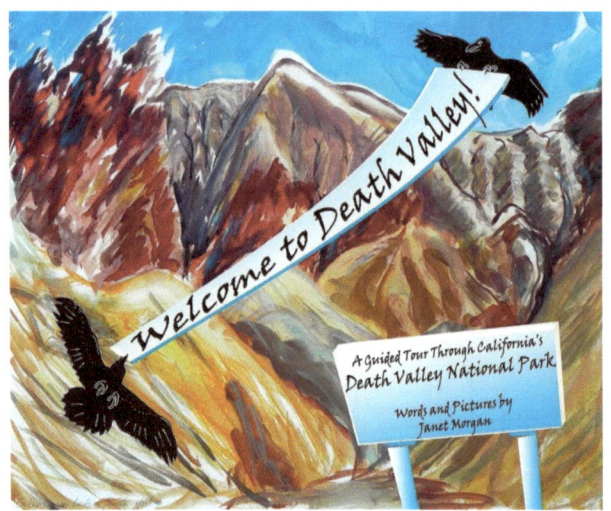

Janet earned her Master of Fine Arts from the University of Wisconsin at Madison, her Bachelor of Fine Arts at the Minneapolis College of Art and Design with a junior year at the Nova Scotia College of Art and Design. She worked for 18 years as an expressive arts therapist with adult cancer patients at Memorial Sloan Kettering Cancer Center in New York City. She has been a full-time artist since 2005.

Janet has had over 100 exhibits and has shown at places including: the Fashion Institute of Technology, the United Nations, the Chapel of Sacred Mirrors and the Jacob K. Javits Federal Building in New York City; the Tabla Rasa Gallery, the Coney Island Museum, the Brooklyn College Library and the Williamsburg Art & Historical Center in Brooklyn; and the Cordova Historical Society and Museum in Cordova, Alaska.

http://artandadventures.com & http://janetmorgan.net/sacredlandscape.html

Brooklyn-based artist **Gregory William Frux** is a realist who finds inspiration in both urban landscapes and wilderness vistas. His cityscapes document and celebrate the life of his city, finding beauty in unexpected places: industrial sites, bridges, vacant lots, the harbor, night scenes and buildings that have seen better days. Starting while in high school, Greg took advantage of art classes at the Brooklyn Museum of Art and the Art Students League; he followed this with a BA in Architecture at City College. He continued his artistic studies at the National Academy and then completed a Masters of Fine Arts at Brooklyn College. He continued painting, honing his skills and deepening his craft, while also working for the Department of Education as an architect and then as curator of a collection of over 1400 works of art. In 2005 he launched his full time artistic career.

Informed and inspired by his mountaineering and back country travel, Frux's wilderness landscapes are diverse in location and climate: the forest and crags of Northeastern United States, the Rocky Mountains, California's Mohave Desert, Alaska, the Yukon, and the Andes of Peru, Bolivia and Patagonia. He has served as artist- in-residence in four National Parks units: Weir Farm National Historic Site in Connecticut, Glacier in Montana, Joshua Tree in Southern California and three times in Death Valley National Park. Along with his partner, Janet Morgan, he has created a large and varied body of work traversing Death Valley, exploring remote desert landscapes and inspiring complex studio work.

In the year 2000, Mr. Frux traveled to Uzbekistan and Kyrgyzstan, where he was one of the first two Americans to show work at the Kyrgyz National Museum of Art. He has worked as an artist aboard ships in Polar Regions north and south, including Arctic Norway in winter and Antarctica. His paintings have been exhibited at Lincoln Center, the Cordova Historical Museum, the American Alpine Club annual dinner, the Coney Island Museum, the Salmagundi Club, Long Island University, Brooklyn College, the Greenwich Arts Council, the offices of HBO and the United States Embassies in Ethiopia and Madagascar. His portrait of author Samuel Delany is on permanent display at New York University. His work is in the collections of the Library of Congress, the American Alpine Club Library, the Metropolitan Transportation Authority, the New York City Board of Education and the National Park Service.

http://artandadventures.com & http://frux.net